Firestorm

ALSO BY JACOB SOBOROFF

Separated: Inside an American Tragedy

Firestorm

The Great Los Angeles Fires and America's New Age of Disaster

Jacob Soboroff

MARINER BOOKS

New York Boston

For information, address HarperCollins Publishers, 195 Broadway, New York, NY 10007. In Europe, HarperCollins Publishers, Macken House, 39/40 Mayor Street Upper, Dublin 1, D01 C9W8, Ireland.

HarperCollins books may be purchased for educational, business, or sales promotional use. For information, please email the Special Markets Department at SPsales@harpercollins.com.

hc.com

FIRST EDITION

Designed by Chloe Foster

Maps by Mapping Specialists, Ltd.

Library of Congress Cataloging-in-Publication Data has been applied for.

ISBN 978-0-06-346796-5

Printed in the United States of America

25 26 27 28 29 LBC 6 5 4 3 2

For my fellow Angelenos

The exponential growth of housing in foothill firebelts, moreover, increases the likelihood of several simultaneous conflagrations and stretches regional manpower reserves to their limit, or beyond. As one national forest official observed: "These fires in Malibu prove that you could throw in every firefighter in the world and still can't stop it."

—Mike Davis, *Ecology of Fear*, 1998

Contents

Part Two

Extended Attack

Los Angeles Wildfires
January 2025

Hurst Fire
Start Date: January 7, 202
Burned Area: 799 acres

Archer Fire
Start Date: January 10, 2025
Burned Area: 19 acres

San Fernand

Kenneth Fire
Start Date: January 9, 2025
Burned Area: 1,052 acres

Palisades Fire
Start Date: January 7, 2025
Burned Area: 23,448 acres

Santa Monica Mountains

Pacific Palisades

Santa Monica

0 8 mi
0 8 km

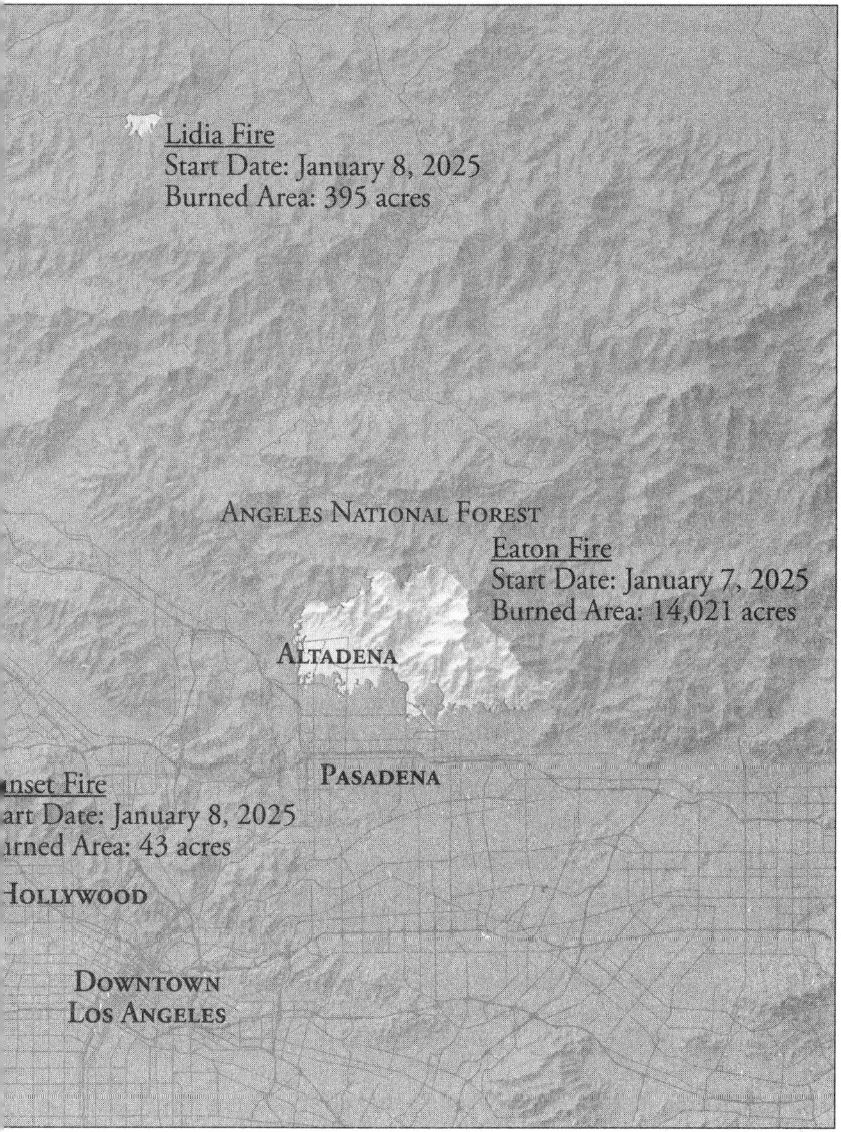

Lidia Fire
Start Date: January 8, 2025
Burned Area: 395 acres

ANGELES NATIONAL FOREST

Eaton Fire
Start Date: January 7, 2025
Burned Area: 14,021 acres

ALTADENA

PASADENA

nset Fire
art Date: January 8, 2025
rned Area: 43 acres

OLLYWOOD

DOWNTOWN
LOS ANGELES

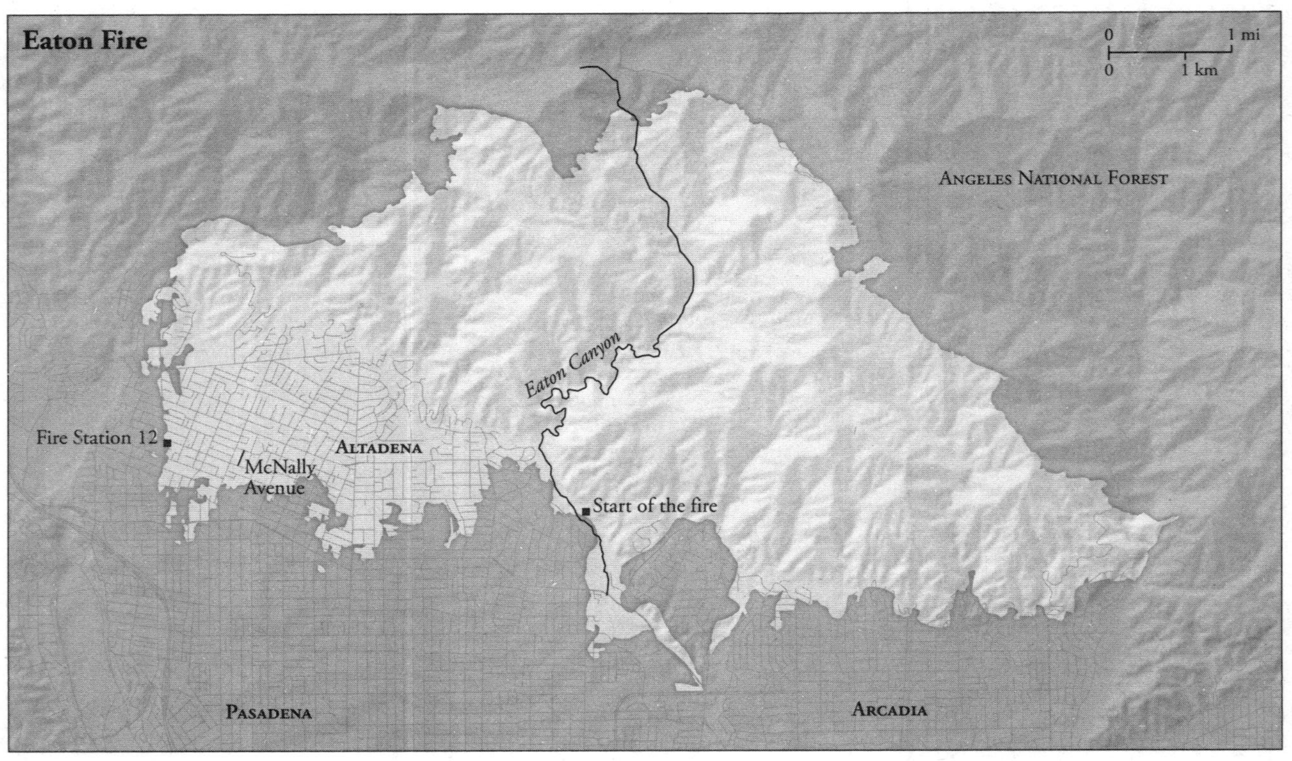
Eaton Fire
0
1 mi
0
1 km
Angeles National Forest
Eaton Canyon
Fire Station 12
Altadena
McNally Avenue
Start of the fire
Pasadena
Arcadia

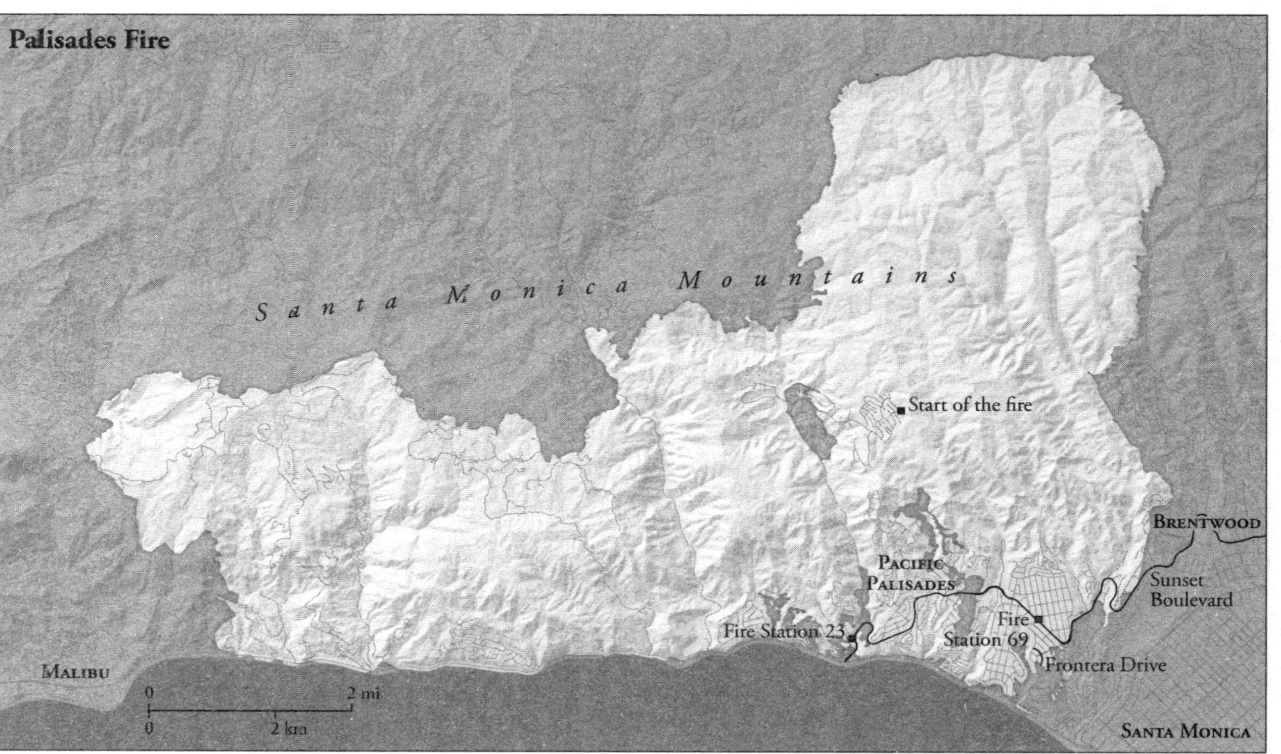
Palisades Fire
Santa Monica Mountains
Start of the fire
Brentwood
Pacific Palisades
Sunset Boulevard
Fire Station 23
Fire Station 69
Frontera Drive
Malibu
Santa Monica
0
2 mi
0
2 km

Author's Note: A Remarkable Time Machine

HERE'S SOMETHING NO JOURNALISM SCHOOL NOR A decade working in all corners of the world will teach you: how to report live on national television while you watch your hometown burn down—essentially wiped off the map. I say that confidently, having just done it. I spent every day for nearly two weeks covering the Great Los Angeles Fires of 2025. The literal firestorm that all Angelenos, including tens of thousands of evacuees, extraordinarily brave first responders, my fellow members of the fourth estate, and I experienced in real time—while you likely followed along with us on television or online—is now one of the most destructive wildfire events in US history.

Fueled by bone-dry conditions and ferocious hurricane-force Santa Ana winds, the Eaton and Palisades Fires burned nearly forty thousand acres, destroyed more than sixteen thousand structures, and killed thirty-one people in the United States' most populous county. The Palisades Fire also happened to burn down the home I was born into, the house my brother, sister-in-law, and soon-to-be-born niece were living in, and virtually the entire community where I grew up including the public park that my parents raised money to renovate in 1986 when I was three. I saw it all incinerate with my own eyes. I chose the cover of this book because photojournalist Ethan Swope, on the fire's first night, captured on El Medio Avenue in the heart of my neighborhood, on a street I drove daily to pick up my high school carpool passengers, what it looked like virtually everywhere across the fire's thirty-seven-square-mile footprint. Beautiful and haunting and dramatic and devastating all at once.

Being there as friends, former neighbors, and so many familiar faces were forced to flee, then to stand there as so many of my childhood memories carbonized while the nation watched was impossible to comprehend in real time. The experience left me with questions that lingered long beyond the fire dominating the headlines. What had I just witnessed? How could it have happened? Is it inevitable something like it will happen again? Those and other questions are why I set out to write this book. What I attempt to do in the pages that follow is, through my own story and those of others who experienced it firsthand—firefighters, fire victims, political leaders, academics, earth scientists, wildlife biologists, meteorologists, and more—to paint as complete a picture as one can of what it felt like to be there, while understanding this was an event experienced in some way by millions.

In the weeks before this disaster unfolded, I virtually begged not to cover fires. It was the example I used when I would tell people what I categorically did not want to report on in late 2024.

"The last thing I want to be doing is covering a fire" was a common refrain, including to my friend Sam on our annual New Year's Eve camping trip while, yes, sitting around a burning fire. "In that ridiculous yellow outfit? Absolutely no way."

Why was I so opposed? Not having to cover fires specifically—

and avoiding what's known as "coverage" reporting more broadly—became a borderline obsession for me. Being part of a coverage team at a news network means that your primary responsibility is to report on *whatever* is happening on any given day. It might be a celebrity trial. Or an ongoing murder investigation. Or a mass shooting. Or the latest natural disaster. And I have many colleagues who are really, really good at that. I am not. And when I have done it, in my mind, those stories were breaking-news detours away from time spent mostly on deeper-dive feature reporting on issues like immigration, inequality, the worst overdose crisis in American history, and election coverage.

When I was hired at MSNBC in 2015, it was explicitly *not* to do day-to-day coverage, and it led to a decade of leading a relatively autonomous work life doing projects that allowed me to carve out a role different from those of so many of my extraordinary colleagues.

"Don't let them change you" was something a senior MSNBC executive said to me more than once.

That kind of idealism was a tough proposition in today's news business. Trust in journalism is at record lows. Newspapers are hemorrhaging subscribers. Television news ratings are declining. And newsroom leaders are shuffling their decks to make these businesses work—and extract maximum profit—for the companies that own them. So, by the end of 2024, it became clear that my professional future was uncertain, even at my own company.

"We'd like you to try working for the LA bureau doing coverage," is how I remember getting the news in 30 Rock from Rebecca Blumenstein, NBC News's president of editorial, in mid-December 2024. I was not thrilled to hear this.

I pushed back, but it was clear this wasn't a choice that was going to be up to me.

"We'll do this for at least three months, and we can reassess after that," she said.

I didn't put up much of a fight: "Sounds good."

So, I walked out of her office a newly minted coverage correspondent. Which is exactly how I ended up sitting at my desk on January 7, 2025, waiting to find out what story I'd be covering next.

These fires, which displaced around 150,000 Angelenos, were not the first major natural disaster or humanitarian crisis I covered in my decade as a broadcast journalist. In 2016 and 2017, I got an up-close look at Hurricanes Matthew and Irma in Florida, and California's Thomas and Skirball Fires. I also had a front row seat to the Trump administration's deliberate and systematic separation of thousands of immigrant families in 2018 and the Biden administration's deportation of a record number of Haitians to the violence-ravaged country in 2021, and spent about three weeks inside Ukraine at the beginning of the war after Russia's full-scale invasion in 2022.

During and after each of these experiences, I would attempt to absorb and share the realities of what I was reporting on and how these "stories" connected to our world and our politics. This work also left me grappling with personal feelings, including sadness, fear, guilt, anger, sense of self, and my connection to and love for my own family. But I have never had a journalistic assignment that so tested me personally and broadened my understanding of America's New Age of Disaster—both natural and humanitarian—as I did in the moment and aftermath of the first working week of 2025.

Fire, it turns out, can be a remarkable time machine, a curious form of teleportation into the past and future all at once.

While I was on the ground in Pacific Palisades, the coastal enclave about twenty miles west of Downtown Los Angeles, every aspect of my childhood flashed before my eyes, and, while I'm not sure I understood it as I stared into the camera as thousand-plus-degree heat melted aluminum in automobiles like it was candle wax, I saw my children's future, too, or at least some version of it. Though that was not immediately clear to me at the time.

Prologue

"I See Smoke"

ACCORDING TO FEDERAL PROSECUTORS, THE COSTLIEST WILDFIRE event in American history was likely started by burning underground roots, a slow-motion ignition that played out over nearly a week. Nestled atop a rugged ridge of the Santa Monica Mountains in Pacific Palisades, California, the hidden danger would have gone overlooked for six days, a remnant of an earlier blaze, the Lachman Fire, named for nearby Lachman Lane, that arose in the earliest moments of New Year's Day 2025. A young man "maliciously" set the initial fire, charges against him allege, the surrounding bone-dry vegetation providing the perfect fuel. Lost in the firefight to stop it, a combustible firebrand—perhaps just a single glowing ember—found a place to hide. Somewhere in or under the beige, cracking soil and the thick, silver-green chaparral that grows from it, that ember ignited the roots below. Soon they would either burn out or flames would find a way to reach the surface again.

The Lachman Fire had startled nearby residents—including my younger brother, Miles, and sister-in-law, Shana, who could smell it from their bedroom as they lay awake, watching the calendar turn to the year their daughter would be born. With a quick attack and minimal wind, it was stopped in its tracks by the Los Angeles Fire Department (LAFD) after burning shy of nine acres. It was contained by sunrise. Or so the department believed.

Firefighter Eric Mendoza of Engine Company No. 69, the crew housed in the heart of the Palisades, battled the fire in his brush gear all night. What a way to spend New Year's Day. He went back to the station for a shift change at six thirty in the morning, relieved by firefighters sent to put out any hot spots. Mendoza would take the next six days off.

For those six days, the underground threat waited patiently, ready to ignite the surrounding brush again. All it might have needed was for a gust of wind to toss the thin layer of soil above it into the air. To give it new life.

On the seventh day, Tuesday, January 7, 2025, the winds shifted, whipping hot air across the surrounding mountaintops, unearthing the burning roots and spreading the fire above ground again. It was just before ten thirty in the morning.

Eric Mendoza was back at work and exercising on the beach with the other firefighters of No. 69, as they do many mornings after reporting for duty. Will Rogers Beach State Park is only a ten-minute drive from their station. His captain, Jeff Brown, looked up in the direction of the Lachman Fire.

"I see smoke," he blurted out.

Even before a call came from dispatch, he mobilized Mendoza and the rest of the company to throw on their brush gear, jump in their vehicles, and head toward the mountains.

"I need thirty, forty, fifty engines right now," Brown called into his radio.

Within minutes, the LAFD's Air Operations Division had

flown to the scene in the turbulent winds, diverting helicopters from a small brush fire that had broken out in the Hollywood Hills in the moments before the Palisades blaze sparked.

"This started up here in 23's district just below the old burn scar," relayed the chopper's pilot to colleagues on the ground, referring to Los Angeles City Fire Station No. 23 and the nineteen acres charred by the Lachman Fire.

"It is pushing directly toward the Palisades and the thing's got a wide path of travel already."

What they were up against would soon have a name: the Palisades Fire.

The 420-horsepower engine roared like a jet taking off as I pressed down on the accelerator, my body banking right but the Jeep Wagoneer veering left on the winding, uphill bend. Personal protective equipment and provisions—some Clif Bars, Coke Zeros, and trail mix—thrown into the second row slid across the floor. This stretch of legendary Sunset Boulevard on the edge of Pacific Palisades came just before the hazardous turn known as "Dead Man's Curve"—one of "the most dangerous spots on Sunset," the *Los Angeles Times* once called it—and I was flooring it.

My left tires crossed over the double yellow line. A crackle came over the two-way radio bouncing around the center cupholder, and my head snapped down to look at it. The staticky voice belonged to NBC News cameraman Jean Bernard Rutagarama, who was following closely behind me.

"What's our secondary exit?" he asked. "Looks like we're getting closer."

Jean Bernard—or J.B.—and I had worked together in high-pressure situations before. It was clear already that this would be another one and that the yellow Nomex fire-resistant jacket and forest-green pants in back might actually come in handy, even vital, instead of using it as TV news cosplay gear. My heart felt like it was pounding as hard as it had when he and I were in Haiti together traveling with humanitarian relief workers in an old Russian-made United Nations chopper to avoid being kidnapped by armed gangs controlling the streets in and around the capital city of Port-au-Prince.

My gaze shot back up as oncoming traffic whizzed past, and I swerved back to the right side of the four-lane road. An hour earlier, at our Universal Studios bureau, my colleague Julia Lee had tossed me the keys to the three-ton white Jeep Wagoneer she'd run out and rented for us while we scrambled to get out the door. A metal placard reading "News Media" bearing the City of Los Angeles's seal rattled on the dashboard. I could see its reflection in the windshield, through which a massive plume of smoke seemed to dominate the entire horizon in front of us, expanding upward and outward as fast as we were barreling toward it.

Grey in front, the smoke cloud was backlit in glowing orange by the sun, which was twenty-five minutes from dipping into the Pacific Ocean behind it. If it wasn't for the catastrophe unfolding in front of us, this was the kind of view, framed by an eclectic hodgepodge of trees you only see in Los Angeles—palm, eucalyptus, pine, and sycamore—that would make it easy to understand why this famous street got its name in 1888.

Tonight there was no beautiful sunset to take in. With my left hand on the wheel as the trees whipped around in my peripheral vision by "a hot wind from the northeast," as writer Joan Didion described the famed and feared Santa Anas, I picked up the walkie-talkie with my right hand to radio back to J.B.

We were charging toward the neighborhood I grew up in. I

didn't need GPS to answer his question about where we should stop as we plowed ahead through a gauntlet of abandoned black, green, and blue plastic bins lining the street on this Tuesday trash day. I pressed down to talk.

"We're going to go into the middle of the Palisades village and stop at Swarthmore," I said. I released my grip and heard two clicks on the mic, shorthand from J.B. acknowledging my transmission. I tossed the radio back down. I was in disbelief.

Is this really happening?

The corner of Swarthmore Avenue and Sunset was an intersection I'd crossed on foot countless times with my parents and siblings and friends throughout my childhood. It sat in the middle of what us locals called "the village" (not to be confused with "Palisades Village," a luxury shopping center developed on the north side of the intersection that opened in 2018). Save one of my four siblings, all of my family had moved out of the Palisades. But Swarthmore and Sunset, around the corner from the former Chinese restaurant that knew us by name, was where I wanted to broadcast from as our hometown went up in flames. I was there only a few days before, ahead of meeting my sister's newborn baby boy.

I had watched images of the chaotic scene earlier in the day from the safety of my office, but I was terrified of what I was about to see as the fire grew. In my passenger seat was producer Bianca Seward, who'd won the unlucky lottery, you could say, of getting paired with me by our bureau chief hours earlier.

We had left the NBC News bureau in the San Fernando Valley. Instead of trying to avoid city traffic by climbing up and over one of the curvy Malibu canyon roads to make our way back south, we stayed with the most direct route. I figured if we got stuck, I could take back streets there. Now, what seemed like seconds from finding ourselves under—or inside—that billowing mass,

Bianca and I sat in an awkward silence until I mustered up the only words I could think of as the smoke dominated ever more of the sky in front of us.

"Fuck, dude."

Bianca didn't respond.

"Fuck," I repeated.

Within minutes, we'd be face-to-face with a massive wall of flames and heat so intense that we'd need to turn around. And within hours, as we witnessed and reported live on a fire explosion no single department could handle, another blaze would erupt in Altadena, the unincorporated community on the other side of Los Angeles County. This one, ultimately more grim and more destructive, became known as the Eaton Fire.

Together, these Great Los Angeles Fires would come to exemplify America's New Age of Disaster, thirteen days before Donald Trump would be sworn in as the forty-seventh president of the United States.

Part One

Initial Attack

1

"This Is Going to Be Horrific"

DAVID GOMBERG IS A FEDERAL WORKER, AN EMPLOYEE of the government of the United States of America. If you live in Los Angeles, he's one of the people behind the forecasts you see on the local news many mornings: a lead forecaster for the National Weather Service's Los Angeles/Oxnard office, part of the National Oceanic and Atmospheric Administration (NOAA), a branch of the US Department of Commerce. He goes by Dave. His youthful energy and lack of wrinkles belie his thirty-two years of full-time work for the weather service. He wears a buttoned-up shirt to the office.

Most of Gomberg's job takes place in a building that could easily be confused for Dunder Mifflin from *The Office*. (Across the street is a real paper factory built in 1969 and now owned by Procter & Gamble.) The National Weather Service facility is a white single-story building in Oxnard, Ventura County, just west of Los Angeles, where work station walls are covered with weather-related papers attached by push pins. On top of the building, antennas stretch into the sky, unless they are blanketed by the dense marine layer from the Pacific Ocean when it creeps in. On the two-hundredth anniversary of NOAA, Gomberg gathered with fellow meteorologists to pose for a photo out front as they celebrated the agency's core mission statement, "Science, Service, and Stewardship."

Gomberg takes raw data that comes in from the automated forecasting systems put in place by the federal government, and converts what would read to most like a foreign language into regular updates—text narratives—that local weather reporters can turn into short snippets to be delivered to the general public.

On Friday, January 3, ninety-six hours before the outbreak of the Palisades Fire, the data he was seeing—across no fewer than four computer monitors at his desk—compelled him and the weather service to issue what's known as a "fire weather watch," alerting the public to the possibility of a wildfire outbreak. Looking at the forecast for wind, relative humidity, and dry fuels moisture, Gomberg understood that action was needed a full day or two earlier than normal. Millions of people could be at risk.

"We wanted to get the word out as soon as possible," the weather expert told me.

That day, spurred by Gomberg's data, California activated its Wildfire Forecast and Threat Intelligence Integration Center (WFTIIC), the integrated hub for wildfire preparedness and response. By Sunday, Gomberg's office issued a red flag warning sooner than they otherwise would, compelling the California Department of Forestry and Fire Protection (Cal Fire) to request and approve the prepositioning of firefighting assets in coordination with local and federal partners.

On the morning of Monday, January 6, it was clear to Gomberg that Los Angeles was staring down the barrel of a potentially deadly event. Inside the National Weather Service office he was spending his fourth straight day of forecasting working alongside Dr. Ariel Cohen, a severe-weather expert from the Midwest.

"This is going to be horrific," Cohen told Gomberg. His concern was based on not only what their advanced computer models were telling them but also a gut feeling from having gone through extreme weather events so many times before. "Something really bad is going to happen."

The data predicted gusts well over sixty miles per hour, combined with a relative humidity of around 10 percent or less, and live-fuel moisture levels at 60 percent or less. The chaparral-covered hillsides of Southern California throughout what they called the wildland-urban interface—the intersection of the natural landscape and cities, were primed to burn. It was clear what they had to do.

At ten in the morning, fire and emergency managers were notified that a normally routine daily one o'clock fire weather call would be important: The weather service would be issuing a "particularly dangerous situation (PDS)" alert, reserved for forecasts of extreme weather that, given the right mix of conditions, could lead to catastrophic outcomes. Gomberg would provide details. The government agency also released a crudely produced graphic that screamed of an impending "LIFE-THREATENING & DESTRUCTIVE WINDSTORM!!!" Much of Los Angeles County was circled in magenta.

After the one o'clock call, at 3:24 p.m., Gomberg personally transmitted the particularly dangerous situation warning, posting it online and sending it directly to the phones of emergency managers throughout the Southland. He'd signed his name at the bottom of the 2,770-word warning, but everything anyone needed to know was on its first page.

URGENT—FIRE WEATHER MESSAGE

National Weather Service Los Angeles/Oxnard CA

324 PM PST Mon Jan 6 2025

. . . PARTICULARLY DANGEROUS SITUATION (PDS) RED FLAG WARNING IN EFFECT NOON TUESDAY UNTIL 4 PM WEDNESDAY DUE TO DAMAGING NORTH TO NORTHEAST WINDS AND LOW HUMIDITIES FOR THE FOLLOWING AREAS: SAN GABRIEL MOUNTAINS / SAN GABRIEL AND SAN FERNANDO VALLEYS (ESPECIALLY FOOTHILLS) / BEVERLY AND HOLLYWOOD HILLS / COASTAL AREAS ADJACENT TO SEPULVEDA PASS / SANTA MONICA MOUNTAINS / SANTA SUSANA MOUNTAINS / MALIBU / EASTERN VENTURA VALLEY (MAINLY NEAR SIMI VALLEY / MOORPARK)—THIS WILL LIKELY BE A LIFE-THREATENING, DESTRUCTIVE, AND WIDESPREAD WINDSTORM . . .

. . . RED FLAG WARNINGS IN EFFECT FOR LOS ANGELES COUNTY AND MUCH OF VENTURA COUNTY—SEE TIMINGS IN HEADLINES BELOW . . .

. . . RED FLAG WARNING IN EFFECT FOR SANTA BARBARA MOUNTAINS INCLUDING EASTERN SANTA YNEZ RANGE TUESDAY INTO WEDNESDAY . . .

THIS IS A PARTICULARLY DANGEROUS SITUATION (PDS) FOR PORTIONS OF LOS ANGELES AND VENTURA COUNTIES!

A very strong, widespread, and destructive north-to-northeast windstorm will bring Extremely Critical fire weather conditions to many areas of Los Angeles and eastern Ventura counties Tuesday afternoon into early Wednesday afternoon. This is a PARTICULARLY DANGEROUS SITUATION (PDS) Red Flag Warning event in many areas, with the combination of very strong upper-level wind support, tightening offshore pressure gradients (LAX-Daggett peaking at -7 to -8 mb), and moderate cold air advection. The strongest winds with this event are expected to be Tuesday afternoon into early Wednesday afternoon when widespread damaging wind gusts of 50 to 80 mph are likely. The San Gabriel Mountains, Santa Susana Mountains, and foothills of the San Gabriel/San Fernando Valleys will likely see areas of destructive wind gusts between 80 and 100 mph! Due to the very strong upper-level wind support and high risk for strong mountain wave activity, typical wind-sheltered areas such as portions of the LA Basin and San Gabriel Valley. The strong winds will likely result in widespread downed trees/power lines, as well as widespread power outages. THIS WILL LIKELY BE THE MOST DESTRUCTIVE WINDSTORM SEEN SINCE 2011 WINDSTORM THAT DID EXTENSIVE DAMAGE TO PASADENA AND NEARBY FOOTHILLS OF THE SAN GABRIEL VALLEY. ANY COMMUNITIES ALONG HIGHWAY 118 AND 210 CORRIDORS WILL BE AT HIGHEST RISK FOR COMPARABLE WIND DAMAGE. Humidity levels are also expected to lower to between 10 and 15 percent in many areas by Tuesday afternoon/evening, potentially lowering into single digits in some areas by late Tuesday night into Wednesday.

> The offshore winds are now expected to arrive early Tuesday morning, resulting in the Red Flag Warning area being moved up to 4 a.m. Tuesday in many areas. AREAS IN A RED FLAG WARNING (ESPECIALLY DURING THE PDS TIME FRAME) WILL HAVE INCREASED RISK FOR LARGE FIRES WITH VERY RAPID FIRE SPREAD, EXTREME FIRE BEHAVIOR, AND LONG RANGE SPOTTING. While the longer duration of strong winds and Red Flag conditions is expected to be focused across Los Angeles and Ventura counties, there is now expected to be a shorter duration of Red Flag conditions across the mountains of Santa Barbara County Tuesday into Wednesday. Long-duration Red Flag Warnings are in effect for much of Los Angeles and Ventura counties Tuesday through Thursday, with Fire Weather Watches in effect Thursday night into Friday.

Now Gomberg and the National Weather Service would begin a constant flurry of consulting with emergency managers and fire agencies. But what nobody could predict, as the alert reverberated across the Southland, was exactly when or how a fire might begin. There was no way for them to know that the Lachman Fire might still be burning below ground. As it did, it perhaps resembled the radiant orange sunsets that sink into the Pacific Ocean that one could see from the ridge on which it was, for now, quietly embedded. As occasional wind gusts howled past, the roots smoldered. The Lachman Fire was still alive.

Ninety-five miles to the southeast, I didn't notice anything amiss. Late that afternoon, I was driving to Orange County, after having spent the morning with my family, who had gathered to celebrate the birth of my newest nephew. I was on my way to see an exhibit about the late Huell Howser, my television idol, at Chapman University.

Huell was the master of talking to everyday people in just about every situation throughout California. Every episode was a journey into a different corner of life and culture. Most of his archive—thousands of hours of television—was donated to the university when he passed away in 2013—including his exploration of fire.

On June 23, 1998, under gloomy skies and clad in that yellow Nomex fire gear, his trademark shades, and a helmet, Howser visited a training session at a controlled burn led by the Los Angeles County Fire Department for female state and county inmates who would be enlisted in firefights. The goal was to instruct them on how to control the grass and brush fires that have terrorized city dwellers and wildland firefighters alike for generations in Los Angeles. Huell's reaction to waist-to-shoulder-high flames, in his trademark Tennessee accent, was as unfiltered as it was honest:

"You know, this is the first time I've even been this close to a fire like this, and this is overwhelming! Look at this!"

"One of the incredible things is you can hear the noise," the county fire official speaking to Huell explained. "Fire creates an incredible amount of noise. And the heat. It starts to heat up, right where we are."

"Oh my gosh!"

He darted over to two female inmates beating back the fire by "cutting a cold trail" with hand tools.

"Ladies, what do you think of this fire this morning?"

"Oh, love!"

"Love it!"

"What do you mean, 'Great, love it'?"

"It's intense," one said, covered in inmate orange fire gear, a neck covering, goggles, and helmet, still holding her hand tool. "That's what we like. We're intense!"

Huell, thrilled to experience the power of the fire, commented on feeling the heat on his face and how mesmerized he was by the skill and techniques of the firefighters.

"This spring burn is one that's been a real eye opener for us," Huell observed later. "It's one we're going to remember for a long time."

It was most definitely not a "particularly dangerous situation." But Huell made everything memorable. It's why I idolize him. He showed a small test fire the same respect as he would the most extraordinary moment you could imagine. It meant something. But I hadn't yet learned that lesson from him, nor from fire.

That night, as I drove home to our house in Los Angeles to give my daughter a bath and put her and her older brother to sleep, the sky was spectacular, a gradient of orange, pink, and blue. I held up my iPhone and took a photo out the window. Palm trees stood at attention, without even a slight breeze, it seemed.

Jake Levine grew up in Pacific Palisades and was back in Los Angeles from Washington, DC, for one of his last acts as a member of the Biden administration. With two weeks to go until Donald Trump would again be sworn in as president, Levine, Special Assistant to the President and Senior Director for Climate and Energy at the National Security Council, was staying overnight at his dad's house before driving to the desert of the Coachella Valley to treat him to a special father-son experience.

President Biden would be dedicating two new national monuments. The one in the desert, Chuckwalla, was something that Jake's father, Mel, a former US congressman, had laid the groundwork for during his tenure on Capitol Hill decades earlier. The next morning, the two of them planned to meet the traveling party from Washington and see President Biden, for whom Jake had traveled the world working on climate issues in the administration.

Jake was my neighbor. We went to Hebrew school together, I drove him and his twin sister, Cara, in our high school carpool, we studied abroad in Paris during college, and we became surfing buddies whenever we both found ourselves at home. We'd usually go out at the point where Sunset Boulevard meets the scenic Pacific Coast Highway. If things went as planned for the Levines, a session wouldn't be out of the question for us when they returned from the desert.

Jake would grab his board from his mom's house on the Palisades bluffs above the Pacific Ocean, we'd catch up about our lives, and joke as we always do about how we two bespectacled, curly haired Jakes are always mistaken for each other.

But things wouldn't go as planned.

"Good Evening," texted Carol Parks, the general manager of the City of Los Angeles's Emergency Management Department, to the city's fire chief, Kristin Crowley, and chief of the Los Angeles Police Department, Jim McDonnell. Their boss, Los Angeles Mayor Karen Bass, was out of the country in Ghana on a diplomatic mission for the Biden administration. In Los Angeles, it was 9:01 p.m. Parks wanted to touch base ahead of both the windstorm forecast by Dave Gomberg and Joe Biden's scheduled visit to Los Angeles. In addition to dedicating those two new national monuments, the president would meet his first great-grandchild.

> Happy New Year and it's my first opportunity to send this Public Safety leadership text. Wishing it could have been on a blue sky day, but duty now calls.

> As you may have seen in emails, the City's EOC [Emergency Operations Center] will be activated at Level 3 (lowest level with EMD staff) beginning at 0800 hours tomorrow and for the duration of this adverse weather event.
>
> Should conditions necessitate us elevating the EOC status, the three of us will need to remain in close contact.
>
> I welcome your input and feedback over the next few days as we lean forward.
>
> Chief McDonnell, EMD will also have staff representation at the POTUS Command Post tomorrow. We are available on-call overnight.
>
> Carol

Two minutes later, the fire chief wrote back.

"Thank you Carol. I'll be available to discuss any necessary actions with the both of you if the need arises. Have a good night."

"Thank you Carol and Kristin," the LAPD chief replied. "I am available anytime. Good night."

2

"Hydrate Up"

AS THE SUN ROSE ON JANUARY 7 IN THE MECCA HILLS Wilderness near California's Coachella Valley, jagged, dry tumbleweeds pushed by the start of the Santa Ana windstorm forecast by the National Weather Service scampered haphazardly past dozens of law enforcement agents from local, state, and federal agencies gathered for an early-morning meeting. They were preparing for President Biden's arrival at what would become Chuckwalla National Monument.

The air temperature had already warmed beyond the customary desert morning chill because of the airflow from the Great Basin, the blasts of air cracking the lips and drying out the cheeks of the agents set to protect the president. They included Riverside County Sheriff's Department deputies dressed in dark green, and cowboy-hatted US Rangers from the Bureau of Land Management wearing tan uniforms with its logo on the shoulder featuring a large pine tree, winding river, and mountain ranges. They and the others were being briefed by the Secret Service, clad in their signature black bulletproof vests emblazoned with a yellow star.

Everyone stood in front of dune buggies as snaggy walls of mountainous rock protruded from the landscape behind them, formed over millions of years of geologic activity around the San

Andreas fault. Today, however, the "Big One," the predicted catastrophic earthquake along the fault, was not the main potential natural disaster on the minds of those assembled. White tents erected as part of a staging area where communication equipment, hauled in Pelican cases by men in suits and crisp white shirts, would be stationed were being ripped from the ground by the increasingly strong Santa Anas. Blue porta-potties that had been hauled out into the desert were swaying side to side. Biden's podium, shrouded under a blue cover, was being pelted with small, sharp sand particles that even the windscreens on the two microphones protruding from its top would not be able to keep from drowning out the president's speech.

A production advance team, including three young men wearing sunglasses—two in all black and the other in shorts and a maroon T-shirt and black ball cap—worked together to prop up a sign marking the day's festivities behind a bulletproof transparent shield. An American flag, draped vertically and set to be lit by no fewer than eight high-powered lights you might see on a movie set, twisted precariously from black scaffolding built for the occasion.

White House staffers, security agents, and members of the media were getting a preview of the "particularly dangerous" windstorm that was on its way to Los Angeles, which seemed increasingly likely to result in the cancelation of the day's festivities.

Around the same time, over 200 miles to the west, Eric Mendoza walked into Fire Station No. 69, serving Pacific Palisades, as he had for the better part of three years. Before that, he'd put in nearly three decades of sterling service as one of the Los Angeles City Fire Department's 3,246 uniformed fire personnel. He had worked in South Central Los Angeles, the San Fernando Valley, East LA, and

Hollywood, but jumped at the opportunity to work in the Palisades when he was tapped to transfer to the exclusive station that he had only visited once fifteen years prior while on overtime.

This isn't real, he thought back then of the picturesque community by the beach with a town square, two supermarkets, a library, a park, and several schools. Of the veteran firefighters who made up the station's crew, he said to himself, "Look at this bunch of old-timers."

By January 2025, Mendoza, who lives with his wife and two teenage daughters in Acton, about an hour away, considered himself one of those old-timers with pride. Firefighters in Los Angeles say the name of their station with an *s* on the end of it—nobody seems to know exactly why—so this station is known as "Sixty-Nines" to the twelve men who showed up before dawn. The other station in the Palisades is "Twenty-Threes."

"The only advice you get when you come to Sixty-Nines is congratulations," he told me.

It's a beautiful firehouse, as perfect as you might picture it. When I was a kid, on Fire Service Day, the fire department's open house, the giant garage door would be pulled up, and they'd let us inside to climb on the engine and into the tiller—the giant truck with the driver up top—and check out the inside of the ambulance. They'd even land an Air Operations chopper across the street in a demonstration that would blow your hat off if you were too close. When I think of the color red, the image that still comes to mind is seeing the shiny trucks in this fire station when I was a young Palisadian.

Mendoza's rank is Firefighter III. He sits in the tiller and controls the rear wheels of the massive engine. On this morning, an hour or so after they arrived for shift change, he and the eleven other men in the station met in the kitchen, as they always do to "lineup" when the station's captain calls for it, ahead of another day in one of Los Angeles's most-coveted firefighting assignments.

"It's pretty much a boys' club sitting around a table," as Mendoza describes it.

By the time they were all in the kitchen to talk about whatever the department sends via e-mail, staffing, overtime, and any major incidents the day before, they could hear the winds kicking up outside, an early taste of what was already happening in the desert to the east.

The afternoon before, the Los Angeles/Oxnard office of the National Weather Service had issued the particularly dangerous situation alert. The lengthy warning, written by David Gomberg, had a section specific to the mountains above Pacific Palisades, stretching all the way across Los Angeles County thirty-seven miles to Altadena, in the foothills of the San Gabriel Mountains.

> Malibu Coast–Western Santa Monica Mountains Recreational Area–
>
> Eastern Santa Monica Mountains Recreational Area–
>
> Western San Fernando Valley–Eastern San Fernando Valley–
>
> Southeastern Ventura County Valleys–
>
> Los Angeles County San Gabriel Valley–
>
> 324 PM PST Mon Jan 6 2025
>
> . . . PARTICULARLY DANGEROUS SITUATION (PDS) RED FLAG WARNING IN EFFECT FROM NOON TUESDAY UNTIL 4 PM WEDNESDAY DUE TO DAMAGING NORTH TO NORTHEAST WINDS AND LOW HUMIDITIES FOR THE FOLLOWING AREAS: SAN GABRIEL AND SAN FER-

NANDO VALLEYS (ESPECIALLY FOOTHILLS) / BEVERLY AND HOLLYWOOD HILLS / COASTAL AREAS ADJACENT TO SEPULVEDA PASS / SANTA MONICA MOUNTAINS / MALIBU / EASTERN VENTURA VALLEY (MAINLY NEAR SIMI VALLEY / MOORPARK) . . . RED FLAG WARNING IN EFFECT FOR ALL OTHER TIMES FROM 4 AM TUESDAY TO 6 PM THURSDAY IN THESE SAME AREAS . . .

. . . FIRE WEATHER WATCH REMAINS IN EFFECT FROM THURSDAY EVENING THROUGH FRIDAY AFTERNOON FOR POTENTIAL WEAK TO MODERATE OFFSHORE WINDS AND LOW RELATIVE HUMIDITY FOR MUCH OF LOS ANGELES AND VENTURA COUNTIES . . .

* WINDS . . . Very strong/damaging north to northeast winds Tuesday into Wednesday, likely peaking in many areas between Tuesday afternoon and Wednesday morning when there is a high risk for strong mountain wave wind activity. During this peak, sustained winds of 35 to 50 mph and widespread damaging gusts of 50 to 80 mph can be expected. Strongest winds likely across the Highways 118 and 210 corridors, including the foothills of the San Gabriel / San Fernando Valleys, and Simi Valley, where very powerful and destructive wind gusts of 80 to 100 mph will be likely. Some particular locations of greatest concern include Sylmar, Porter Ranch, San Fernando, Burbank, Glendale eastward to foothill communities such as La Crescenta, Altadena, Monrovia, Pasadena, Azusa, and Glendora. Moderate north to northeast winds will likely persist Thursday with gusts of 30 to 50 mph, with some weakening possible by Friday.

> * RELATIVE HUMIDITY . . . Humidities 20 to 30 percent early Tuesday morning, falling to 10 to 20 percent by late Tuesday afternoon/evening. Humidities will potentially fall to single digits in some areas from Wednesday into Friday.
>
> * IMPACTS . . . If fire ignition occurs, conditions are favorable for very rapid fire spread and extreme fire behavior, including long-range spotting, which would threaten life and property. There will be a high risk for widespread downed trees and power lines, as well as widespread power outages.
>
> PRECAUTIONARY/PREPAREDNESS ACTIONS . . .
>
> A Red Flag Warning means that critical fire weather conditions are either occurring now, or will shortly. Use extreme caution with anything that can spark a wildfire. Residents near wildland interfaces should be prepared to evacuate if a wildfire breaks out. See readyforwildfire.org and wildfirerisk.org for information.
>
> A Fire Weather Watch means that critical fire weather conditions are likely to occur in the coming days. Residents near wildland interfaces should prepare now on what to do if a wildfire breaks out. See readyforwildfire.org and wildfirerisk.org for information.

The men of Sixty-Nines were clocking the potential danger; brush fires weren't regular occurrences, but they happened in the Palisades. And they knew what to do. As a kid, I evacuated once from a house we lived in up in the Santa Monica Mountains, but it felt very precautionary. These guys were on it.

"Hey, hydrate up," they advised one another. "Make sure your packs are ready. Make sure everything's on the rig like it's supposed to be."

Tuesday was one of the three days that Mendoza would work a twenty-four-hour shift this week before getting the customary four days off. He and his fellow firefighters on duty finished their meeting in the kitchen, and most of them piled into what Mendoza calls the pump (the truck with the permanently mounted water pump), the truck (the ladder truck), and the rescue (which has specialized equipment for rescue scenarios) and made the short drive down Temescal Canyon Boulevard—one of three connecting roads between the foothills of the Santa Monica Mountains and the beach in the Palisades—to the Pacific Coast Highway for some morning exercise, ready to deploy at a moment's notice.

3

"I Need Thirty, Forty, Fifty Fire Engines"

BEFORE I LEFT FOR WORK, MY NINE-YEAR-OLD SON, Noah, told me to look outside. Strong wind gusts were twisting the olive trees that line our front yard and, overgrown as they were, causing them to shed their narrow leaves. Thick pine needles, too, were drifting from a tree in our neighbor's yard over our fence. *That's going to make a mess*, I thought, but not much more as I headed out.

I pulled into the parking garage we use at Universal Studios—named for the famed comic duo Abbott and Costello—then walked up a ramp, across a manicured courtyard, and into the NBC News Los Angeles Bureau. It was breezy enough that I came into work wearing a jean jacket, but not unusually so. I figured today would be another slow day after the holiday for me, with Monday having been dominated by my Washington, DC, colleagues' coverage of the anniversary of the January 6, 2021, attack on the US Capitol and the certification of the 2024 election. Now the funeral of President Jimmy Carter was central to much of the day's live coverage.

On this Tuesday morning I was back at my desk, a cubicle filled with reminders of assignments past. Playing on the small television that hangs over its upper-right corner was President-elect Trump, who had just commenced a news conference from Mar-a-Lago, his Florida estate and club. The Trump-Vance campaign sign adorned the front of the lectern, and multiple American flags provided his backdrop.

"Thank you very much. It's an honor to be with you. Many things are happening that are exciting, very exciting for our country, and we're honored to welcome one of the most respected business leaders in the Middle East, indeed the world," Trump said before introducing Hussain Sajwani, an Emirati billionaire who helped develop the Trump International Golf Club in Dubai.

Sajwani, at Trump's invitation, stepped to the microphone and announced an investment of $20 billion, which he said he'd been waiting to do for the last four years, to build a data center in the United States, drawing praise from the president-elect.

"And that man knows what he's doing. He knows. So Hussain, we're going to work with you and make sure everything goes smoothly. We have powers that haven't really been used in terms of environmental."

I was half paying attention. My mission for the morning was to try to figure out stories I could pitch to my bosses and get bought in this first workweek of the new year that would keep me out of the "coverage" rotation. I heard Trump start talking about windmills.

"The blades, they take three ships to ship them. It's crazy. They're dangerous. You see what's happening up in the Massachusetts area where they had two whales wash ashore in I think a seventeen-year period, and now they had fourteen this season. The windmills are driving the whales crazy, obviously."

My eyes darted up at the screen. I turned up the volume.

"And I don't know if you've ever gone to Palm Springs, California, or any of these places where you have long term windmills standing," the president-elect said. "They're a disaster."

Immediately, I sensed a story. I know those windmills. I've driven by them a million times as I've gone out to Palm Desert to visit my late grandmother, and now my parents, who spend much of their time there. *I should do that,* I thought. I kept searching for contact information of Palm Springs officials, private businesses, and federal offices that could help me do a reality check on what these windmills really did and what they looked like. The first person I got on the phone was a public relations official from Southern California Edison, better known as SoCal Edison, whose transmission lines carry much of the energy generated by the wind power.

When the PR man told me he had to call me back because of a "wind event," it didn't even register with me what might be going on in the exact part of Southern California I had reached out to him about. I had my headphones on for the call, so I didn't notice the commotion going on around me in the office. I kept digging for sources who could help me get to the bottom of Trump's claims about windmills.

The sitting president of the United States, Joe Biden, was in Los Angeles getting ready to travel to the Coachella Valley. His destination was about an hour past the windmills on the way to Palm Springs that President-elect Trump was railing on and on about, to dedicate the Chuckwalla National Monument, "where the Mojave and Colorado Deserts intersect, ancient trails weave through a land of canyon-carved mountain ranges bound together by radiating alluvial bajadas and dark tendrils of dry wash woodlands," as the proclamation establishing it would ultimately say.

President Biden was set to meet local leaders, as well as California Governor Gavin Newsom and Secretary of the Interior Deb Haaland, the first Native American cabinet secretary in our country's history, at a place where Biden would later say in his statement "imprints of generations of Indigenous peoples are found throughout the region in the trails, tools, habitation sites, and spectacular petroglyphs and pictographs they left behind." But after gathering the traveling press at 9:25 a.m. for an early departure, reports came in from the Coachella Valley about the dust and whipping wind that the White House team on the ground were taking to the face. The conditions had forced a delay in the motorcade's departure from Los Angeles to Chuckwalla, as Danny Kemp of Agence France-Presse communicated in his pool report.

> Out of town pool report #1—Delay
>
> Good morning from Los Angeles. Just to flag some scheduling changes for POTUS' trip to designate two new national monuments in remarks in Box Canyon, California. The White House says it is due to weather issues.
>
> In updated guidance issued early this morning, the departure from the RON [rest over night] was originally brought forward to 9:25 a.m., but after loading the motorcade, pool was told there was a delay and pool is now holding at the RON as of 10:10 a.m.
>
> Will update when we know more.

Jake and Mel Levine were en route to the event after an early-morning departure from LA, when they received a phone call from Sam Levy, an advance man to the president. Levy, who was set to meet them upon their arrival, gave Jake a heads-up that things were looking dicey on the ground because of the tempestuous weather.

That call was followed by word from another White House staffer that the event would likely be canceled. My friend Jake's wife, the journalist Jacqueline Alemany, was expecting. Not only that, he had just days to wrap up his work at the White House. Instead of spending the day in the desert, Jake turned around near some outlet malls outside of Palm Springs and headed back to Los Angeles with his dad, both of them disappointed.

The next morning, Jake was scheduled to lead his final Interagency Policy Committee meeting and the agenda would focus on Ukraine. So, he booked an early-afternoon flight to get back to the White House instead of taking the red-eye.

As Governor Gavin Newsom waited for Biden to arrive at Jacqueline Cochran Regional Airport in Thermal, California—not far from the annual Coachella music festival—his phone rang, too. It was Biden, who still hadn't left his Los Angeles hotel.

"Hey, pal," the president said, "I just want you to take a look at this." He was referring to video of the white tents blowing away earlier in the morning. Young staffers, their suits caked in desert dust, clearly wouldn't be able to guarantee the images of a resolute president pushing through the elements to dedicate America's newest national monument. "You know, I really want to make this happen."

"Mr. President, I appreciate it. Don't come down. This is crazy. This makes no sense."

Biden felt badly that everyone had taken the time to get down to the desert to pre-position and pitched Newsom on an alternate event in Los Angeles.

"We'll do anything you want," Newsom told the president, as they agreed that the dedication would be canceled.

Newsom now had time to kill in the desert as his team scrambled to come up with a plan. The governor and his aides stopped at a Starbucks on Cesar Chavez Street in Coachella to figure out whether he should fly back to the state capital of Sacramento from the airport there, in the shadow of Mount San Jacinto.

"Let's just drive up to LA, and we'll have more flight options," Newsom suggested, "to leave out of LAX. And it's an opportunity as well just to check in with the president if he's available personally."

Will Rogers Beach is just over a mile and a half from Sixty-Nines, the fire station in the heart of the Palisades. A full mile of that is the drive down the long slope of Temescal Canyon Road, which connects Sunset Boulevard and the Pacific Coast Highway. In high school, I was heading home on Temescal in my mom's car when a vehicle suddenly made a U-turn in front of me. Unable to stop, I T-boned the other car, flipping it over onto its roof. Not a great day.

Temescal runs along Palisades Charter High School, a massive thirty-four-acre campus home to nearly three thousand students. We all call it Pali. Every Fourth of July in the Palisades starts with a running race, then a parade through town, and finally a massive fireworks show launched from Pali's football field.

At the bottom of Temescal, across PCH, is Lifeguard Tower 14, one of 158 iconic sky-blue "towers" that dot a vast expanse of flat sand that stretches for three miles on 103 acres. *Los Angeles* magazine once described the lifeguard towers as resembling "mini midcentury modern stilt houses or the most seaside of seaside cabins." This is where they filmed *Baywatch*. Sometimes when you'd pass by the lifeguard station there—a much bigger structure—it was surrounded by production equipment and trailers. And somewhere in there were Pamela Anderson and David Hasselhoff.

This location was also where the men of Sixty-Nines parked their fire trucks and went for a back-and-forth beach run Tuesday as the sun rose from behind the Santa Monica Mountains and started to warm the Pacific coastline, while one member of the company stayed back as truck security. They always made sure to go only as far as you could see the rigs. From the beach, you also have a clear shot of the mountains above, which was the view Mendoza had as he walked on the windy beach following his workout.

At the top of those mountains, the wind was even more fierce, causing the smoldering roots hidden below the Lachman Fire's remnants to hiss and pop. Its heat radiated outward as the soil above it was blown away, making contact with the whooshing Santa Ana gusts. Suddenly flames reached upward and outward as the fire that burned a week prior was now raging again.

Whatever around that hadn't burned on New Year's morning quickly began to ignite, and within minutes, what could have been mistaken from the beach as part of the drifting clouds above on a beautiful blue-sky day became easily identifiable as brown smoke, billowing upward from the spreading flames below, now sucking oxygen off the hillside and with it, incinerating chaparral and creating a thick, grey layer above, clearly distinct from the white clouds.

"I see smoke," observed Captain Jeff Brown, the leader of Sixty-Nines since 2018.

Mendoza looked up, in the same general direction as the fire he'd fought on the last day he worked: New Year's morning. He and his crew abruptly threw on all their gear: jacket, helmet, pants, fireproof boots, and a fire shelter kit strapped to their backs in case they were overcome by flames. Then they hopped in their trucks, turned on their sirens, and headed up the hill.

Over the radio, Mendoza heard Captain Brown call for backup: "Hey, I need thirty, forty, fifty fire engines right now."

Within thirty minutes of his motorcade's drive to Los Angeles, Gavin Newsom's phone went off. It was Ann Patterson, his cabinet secretary, calling to relay that there was a newly ignited brush fire burning in Los Angeles—around twenty or thirty acres. Newsom, who had been to the scene of dozens of wildfires in his six-year tenure as governor, decided to go see it for himself. In November 2018, shortly after winning the gubernatorial election, the governor-elect visited the Northern California town of Paradise, where at least eighty-five souls perished in the deadliest fire in the state's history.

Like the Santa Anas fueling the blaze he was en route to see, Newsom raced west on a multi-hour drive—his car rocking as it headed past the same windmills that President-elect Trump had been eviscerating early in the morning—to see yet another wind-driven wildfire.

On his right, with thirty miles to go before he arrived in the Palisades, he would pass the San Gabriel Mountains, the community of Altadena below, and a set of high-voltage power lines in Eaton Canyon. While not yet part of the unfolding catastrophe, they would be in the hours to come.

4

"I Should Go"

EVEN BEFORE THE FIRST 911 DISPATCH REACHED THE firefighters of Sixty-Nines, the company was en route from its workout routine along the Pacific Coast Highway to the Palisades Highlands neighborhood. Halfway there, to be exact—about two miles. Eric Mendoza, sitting in the tiller, making sure the back wheels of the massive engine were navigating the long, windy, uphill roads—from sea level to around two thousand feet—was hatching a game plan.

We need to figure out a place with the companies that we have, he thought. No use going into the brush—the dry, already-engulfed chaparral behind the homes. They'd call Los Angeles City Fire Air Operations as backup for that.

Structure protection would be the objective.

When they arrived on scene, they were alone under billowing smoke, with flames licking up Santa Ynez Canyon toward some of the hundreds of homes developed in the secluded mountain community that had been master-planned in the 1970s. The fire looked to be originating from the same place near Topanga State Park, where Mendoza and his company beat back the fire on New Year's Day.

"These homes," Captain Jeff Brown signaled to his men about

the nearby properties they would be defending. "The fire's coming this way."

The men of Fire Station No. 69 were used to battling brush fires in the Santa Monica Mountains. It was part of the job and part of the territory working in the wildland-urban interface of Pacific Palisades. They started pulling hoses through residents' backyards and waited for the fire to approach—up a canyon toward their position—so they could attack as the winds kicked up.

As the fire burned, pushed in all directions by the gusting Santa Anas, Sixty-Nines fought back, extinguishing the blaze directly in front of them. It seemed like things were under control.

"Let's take a picture!" one of them shouted. A selfie, as they knocked down another potentially catastrophic Los Angeles wildfire.

Click.

The men of Twenty-Threes, the other fire station in the Palisades, which is situated just up Sunset Boulevard from its intersection with Pacific Coast Highway, were elsewhere in the Highlands. The area is their "first-in," or jurisdiction, and they were dispatched at the same time Sixty-Nines rushed up from the beach. They had a slight head start, so they ended up around where it was first reported—near Chastain Parkway and Piedra Morada Drive.

Tim Larson, thirty-five years on the job with the Los Angeles Fire Department and four with Twenty-Threes, was an old hand at brush fires as a former hotshot working for the US Forest Service in the Angeles National Forest, across Los Angeles County. When he and his engine arrived at the reporting address, they blew past it because they could see the fire on the side of the hill. They made a U-turn and ended up in a cul-de-sac of mansions on Calle Victoria, backing the rig in just in case they needed to peel out, and hooked up to a fire hydrant. As Twenty-Threes fought to save the handful of homes there, the men of Sixty-Nines were wrapping up what they thought was their initial attack on what was now being called the Palisades Fire.

"We've got the fire under control. We've got the helicopters coming," Mendoza recalls leadership saying, while looking down at a valley turned black—a sign there was nothing left to burn in the area. From the backyards of the multi-thousand-square-foot homes in the Highlands, Mendoza thought it might be time to wrap up and head home.

A call came through on the radio: Structures were burning on the other side of the canyon, out of sight.

Mendoza called his two daughters. "I'm at a brush fire; just letting you know. Love you guys. If I don't pick up, it's because I'm busy."

He snapped another photo and sent it. It was the last time they'd hear from him for days.

My phone pinged at 10:55 a.m. It was a text from my brother, Miles, on the group chat I share with my parents, my four siblings, my wife, my two brothers-in-law, and my sister-in-law. He was on the other side of the canyon from Sixty-Nines and Twenty-Threes—where the radio call indicated fire was now burning.

"Big Palisades fire," he wrote. "We are evacuating."

The blaze had engulfed the hillside above his in-laws' home, where he and my pregnant sister-in-law, Shana, were living as they renovated their first home—just down the hill—ahead of the birth of their daughter. Winds had pushed the smoke, and the smell of the mountain burning, into the house. It was as if a barbeque had been lit inside.

"Really bad."

"stay safe," my sister Molly wrote, followed by two heart emojis.

"yes be safe," my sister Hannah seconded, inviting them to her home in Brentwood, seven and a half miles away. "come here if u need."

My dad and other sister, Leah, also chimed in, inviting them to their respective places.

Shana echoed my brother: "Really bad."

"Coming," my brother wrote.

With that text, he attached a photo: a dark-grey, almost-black plume rising near the house, an umbrella of smoke towering over everything they owned.

"This was 5 mins after it started. Much worse now."

I changed the channel from MSNBC to the local news. KNBC began its eleven o'clock newscast with an ominous voice-of-God open: "NBC 4 News at Eleven a.m. starts with breaking news!"

"LIFE-THREATENING WINDSTORM," warned the big breaking-news banner at the bottom of the screen as images of dust and debris rolled through the frame. Anchor Annabelle Sedano cut to the chase: "A brush fire is burning in Pacific Palisades. Right now it's about two acres, and look at that! You can see that dark plume of smoke right there. Here's a look at how strong the winds have been this morning, and the gusts are only going to intensify."

Just then a burst of dark-red and orange flame became visible in the center of the screen—on the ridge of the mountain where my brother lived.

I texted him back.

"Yeah I'm watching on TV, everyone talking about it in the newsroom here," I typed, following up with some intel I had overheard in the background: "2 air tankers being deployed there."

According to an on-screen graphic displaying wind gusts around the area, Los Angeles International Airport, about twenty miles south of the Palisades, was reporting winds of thirty miles per hour. Sedano repeated that the fire was two acres in size, but I knew that couldn't be true based on what I was seeing. The size of the plume and the explosive flames below it looked absolutely massive. They were dancing—whipping—in all directions directly above what I thought was the street I had lived on from age ten until I graduated high school.

Holy fucking shit was the thought going through my head. *Holy fucking shit.*

As the camera, positioned at the airport, zoomed out, it sure didn't look to me like a brush fire burning in the distance beyond freeways and over homes and with the communities of Santa Monica and Westwood and the Palisades in between. It looked like a bomb had been dropped on the Santa Monica Mountains. The smoke stretched across the entire panoramic view, blowing out toward the ocean to the west.

"I'm just getting a bit of information from our producer now that this fire was at two acres—it's now grown to twenty acres," anchor Sedano said, sounding somewhat nervous. Hard not to be watching what was playing out. It had been only five minutes since the broadcast began. I stood up and looked over my cubicle and said to anyone who would listen that I knew exactly what we were looking at and exactly where it was.

"My brother lives right there—I grew up right there—he's evacuating now. This is my neighborhood!" I probably sounded pretty frantic. I wasn't sure if anyone was really paying attention to what I was saying, and they weren't, actually. What they *were* doing was getting ready to dispatch, or "launch," bureau correspondents out to the fires. I wasn't one of them. I was glued to my little smartTV. Even on the superwide shot, you could see the glow of the flames.

The meteorologist, Stephanie Olmo, said what I was thinking: This fire was definitely going to keep growing. Anyone who took even an occasional hike, as we Angelenos are fond of doing, knew that instead of returning with boots or sneakers caked in mud, as one might this time of year, a thick layer of dust was more likely, the sign of a bone-dry start to winter.

"So far this water season, we've only picked up about a tenth of an inch of rain," she explained. "Typically around this time, we should be well above that. Right? So we have a lot of dry, dry vegetation. It could easily ignite. It could spread quickly, especially with the type of wind speed that we have out there."

As she was talking, the camera pushed back in, so that homes looked a stone's throw from the inferno. Now on the phone was Fire Chief Sam DiGiovanna, the network's fire expert and a thirty-five-year veteran of the fire service.

"This is more than twenty acres at this point. This fire is moving at a very rapid rate of spread. The fuel moisture content is at the lowest it can be. So the tiniest spark can start a fire—and you think of all the embers that are blowing ahead of this fire. The big concerns I see right now with this are these homes to the southwest of this fire, right in the path of this fire."

He was talking about where my brother and his family lived, now completely awash in the hazy smoke, the thick scent of burning vegetation filling the nostrils of those who had stayed behind.

"And this is just what we *don't* want," DiGiovanna continued. "This is just the beginning of these couple days of this wind event. We start getting multiple fires, we're going to start losing resources."

What the chief said next freaked me out.

"These people in the path of this fire right now, even if they have not been told to evacuate, they should be evacuating."

I texted our group chat a photo of the television screen I was watching, asking for an update.

"Really bad," my brother wrote again. "We all left."

Manhattan Beach, about twenty-five miles south of Pacific Palisades, is situated on the southern edge of Santa Monica Bay—not a hotspot for brush fires—but the wind event that was playing out made Manhattan Beach Fire Department firefighter James Stratton, who drives his company's fire engine, eager to get ready for whatever was to come.

"Let's go get the quick-attack lines. Let's pull the tent," he said to his captain that morning. By the time the Palisades Fire started, texts were flying from colleagues in other agencies.

Get ready. You're probably coming.

By eleven thirty, they were out the door, racing up the 405 Freeway, and Stratton saw the header of the fire for the first time. With nineteen years of firefighting under his belt, he gave his crew some advice:

"We're in for it. Be ready."

The whole sky was consumed by an enormous plume of smoke. Big and brown. As fast as they were driving, the smoke looked to be moving at a similar clip, with the wind out over the Pacific Ocean. The fire was growing.

Stratton knew it was going to be a long day. He looked at his captain and told him to take video of what they were seeing.

"Shoot this. You're never gonna see this again."

Once they made their way to PCH through the McLure Tunnel, Stratton felt like what he was seeing was surreal—as if he were in a disaster movie.

Super Scoopers off to his left, flying in tandem, coming across and going down into the Pacific Ocean to pick up water. He told the rookie on his engine the same thing he told his captain earlier.

"Shoot this. These are moments you don't see. Oh my God! Look how big this is!"

At 11:31 a.m., another update from Danny Kemp, the journalist traveling with President Biden, that reflected his earlier conversation with Governor Newsom: "From the White House: Due to weather issues, the president will not travel to Thermal, CA." The president, who had entered his fortified limousine known as the Beast, at 10:58 a.m., stepped out of it about ten minutes later, and walked back into his Century City hotel, Kemp reported.

The message came through to my work email, which I was monitoring while watching the fire continue to spread, glued to the local news. Karma Dickerson, a reporter from the local NBC station, made her way to the intersection of Sunset Boulevard and Palisades Drive, at the bottom of the hill that Eric Mendoza and his team had raced up less than an hour before. Joining by phone, she described a chaotic scene where she stood looking at terrified residents, stuck in their cars with nowhere to go, desperate to outrun the smoke and flames moving down the mountains toward the Pacific Ocean. Fire trucks arriving from other parts of Los Angeles couldn't get through, either, and their sirens were deafening.

"Honestly, pure pandemonium," she reported. "And I don't say that lightly. Getting in here—traffic is bumper-to-bumper. People in a panic of trying to escape the areas farther north have taken over both lanes of traffic," she said of Palisades Drive, the only way in and out of the Highlands—other than a fire road that was engulfed in flames.

As a smoke alarm blared in the background, she continued to report by phone. Meanwhile, the photojournalist who'd accompanied her had moved higher up into the mountains and was shooting the advancing edge of the flames. Based on the onscreen images, it looked to me like the street that my brother and his wife were living on, shrouded in dark-brown smoke. Cars flowed downhill while fire engines drove up. Engines from stations over the city rolled past: Threes, Ninety-Eights, Fives, Seventeens, Forty-Ones.

"All around us," Dickerson said, "we see people with their dogs, they're running. You see people with suitcases that are walking down the road because you can't move. Traffic isn't moving, so people are doing what they can to get out. Just walking themselves out."

As she spoke, another update from the reporter traveling with President Biden hit my inbox at 12:08 p.m. "From the White House: Today's event will be rescheduled for next week at the White House so that key stakeholders can attend," Danny Kemp relayed. "For information, we're currently seeing high winds in LA."

The "high winds" described in the White House pool report were ripping through and down Santa Ynez Canyon, carrying with them embers that were causing palm trees on the median to ignite like matchsticks.

With panic overtaking residents, Dickerson watched. A civilian wearing a short-sleeve collared shirt, blue shorts, and sneakers approached an LAFD vehicle marked Command 42. Unsuccessfully trying to drive it uphill was an assistant chief—a senior incident commander for large-scale crises like this one.

"Tell me how I can help," the man said earnestly. "Direct cars out of here?"

"Just tell LAPD people are running for their lives," replied the assistant chief. "Open it up. Free flow. Whatever it takes."

"Yep, yep!"

The firefighter turned around and got back in the driver's seat of his car. But wedged in by vehicles on both sides—a Jeep and a Porsche directly to his left, a Toyota on the sidewalk to his right, and a line of cars as far as the eye could see up into the dark-brown smoke rolling down Palisades Drive toward Sunset Boulevard—he wasn't going anywhere.

At 12:18 p.m., Anthony Marrone, the Los Angeles County fire chief, texted a photograph from a beach vantage point toward the Los Angeles fire to three of his colleagues: LAFD Chief Kristin Crowley, whose jurisdiction the fire was in; Dustin Gardner, chief of the Ventura County Fire Department, to the west; and Brian Fennessy, the Orange County Fire Authority chief, to the south. Together they were responsible for the lives of millions of people across Southern California. The photo showed another angle of the billowing smoke, now wider and darker and more expansive, a ragged stain in the azure sky.

"Not good," Marrone wrote.

"No," replied Crowley.

"Not at all," added Gardner.

"Oh, man," said Fennessy.

With the mutual-aid effort well underway, Crowley pleaded for help.

"Anything else you can send us, we will take it. Starting to lose homes and people trapped."

The chiefs signaled that everything at their disposal—strike teams, hand crews, aircraft, and more—was en route. They would report to a command post established at Will Rogers Beach.

On television, the scenes were reminiscent of evacuations from Lower Manhattan during September 11, 2001—another tragedy I had the misfortune of witnessing personally in my first week as a freshman at New York University. Angelenos were running, suitcases and pets and children and elderly relatives in tow, dispersing in all directions, smoke and embers chasing them as they attempted to escape. A nightmare playing out in daylight.

Down on the Pacific Coast Highway, where Eric Mendoza and the men of Sixty-Nines had left an hour before, another KNBC crew, with correspondent Alex Rozier in the passenger seat, was in the lone vehicle heading up. By a quarter after twelve, it made it to the corner of Temescal and Bowdoin Street, where, for as long as I can remember, the painted wall on the southwestern side of the intersection depicted a scene of the native inhabitants of the Palisades: the Chumash and Tongva people.

The Santa Anas blowing through the Santa Monica Mountains were gusting upward of fifty miles per hour, sending a cloud of ash over two yellow Los Angeles Unified School District busses, heading in the same direction as reporters crawling toward the worst of the fire that had started less than two hours before. Fire engines arrived from other jurisdictions, including Beverly Hills, as part of a mutual-aid effort.

At 12:22 p.m., I was still at my desk, biting my nails. Rozier had begun a live report from the car as an LAPD SUV with lights and sirens blaring attempted to split the traffic and drive up the middle of the road. On the screen, I recognized the synagogue that our family attended when we lived there, Kehillat Israel, or KI for short. Kids were streaming out of the preschool I had attended, running away from the looming fire, in the opposite direction Rozier was driving. I again texted my family group chat with a photo of what I was watching.

"KI on the right. Looks like a total shitshow on Sunset."

I got up from my desk and walked into the office of the bureau chief, Polly Powell.

"Polly—I should go. I grew up in the Palisades."

She explained that three other correspondents were already on their way and that there wasn't an available camera crew. But she was going to look into it. In the meantime, she asked my colleague Julia Lee to run out and pick up a rental car we could take there if need be.

"Do you have your fire gear?"

"I don't, sorry."

I didn't tell her I had jammed it into the bottom of my storage unit because of my feelings about covering fires. She called downstairs to make sure there was extra gear. There was.

5

"As Bad as It Can Get"

NOTHING WAS STOPPING THE PALISADES FIRE. IT WAS belching out of garage door windows and palm tree canopies and car hoods, sending residents, including my own family, fleeing before the eyes of 5,835,790 television households in the Los Angeles media market. Ash was raining down like snowflakes, and embers were flowing horizontally at the base of Palisades Drive below the Highlands and, on the other side of the Santa Ynez Canyon, above the Marquez Knolls neighborhood where I had spent many evenings eating Italian food under the red awning of Vittorio's.

There, on a ridge overlooking a winding canyon divided by Bienveneda Avenue, is where my brother and his wife lived with her parents as their own home was under construction at the bottom of the hill. On the opposite side of Bienveneda is where our family had lived—on another ridge overlooking the Pacific Ocean. We could see my future sister-in-law's house from our own.

All of that was now under a choking layer of particulate so thick it was visible on KNBC's radar as a constant stream of white moving from northeast to southwest, the Los Angeles coastline made to look like a chimney spout. Winds were gusting upward of sixty miles per hour. Battalion 706, from the northeast San

Fernando Valley, about as far away as you can get from the Palisades within the four corners of the City of Los Angeles, arrived on scene and bobbed and weaved its way around the obstacles of abandoned cars on both sides of the street. By 12:39 p.m., the fire had consumed over two hundred acres of the Santa Monica Mountains, the radiant heat and embers gobbling up homes on the fire's flank and creating new spot fires farther downwind.

That was no doubt clear to the Los Angeles Fire Department Air Operations unit, which had started the day by dispatching every available aircraft—the LAFD has five Leonardo AW139 twin-engine helicopters and two Bell 505 single-engine choppers—to a small brush fire in the Hollywood Hills, where they could see the "loom up," or smoke column, of the Palisades Fire.

Van Nuys Airport, where LAFD Chief Pilot Dan Child was monitoring conditions, is around 800 feet above sea level, and the mountain range between there and the Palisades Fire is about 2,000 feet. Pilots leaving from there would move along what's known as the Bull Creek route—a waterway running through the San Fernando Valley that feeds into the Los Angeles River—then traveling south over the Santa Monica Mountains, at around 1,300 feet, they could see the 1,000-foot smoke column from the Palisades. Listening to radio traffic back at headquarters, Child knew it was going to be a long run. He recalled every available pilot to report to duty. At 12:42 p.m., a fixed-wing water-dropping aircraft swooped down from the east, diving down into the smoke cloud over the Palisades, and disappeared into darkness.

At the same time, from the ground on Lachman Lane, around the corner from where my brother lived, some firefighters from Twenty-Threes had moved to the ridge across from the Highlands. They were dousing homes that had already burned to the ground. Suddenly blue sky peeked through—for a moment. Across the street, a newly ignited home was spewing dark-black smoke; the wind shifted it and quickly darkened the sky again. Engines from Ninety-Eights, Seventeens, and Fives drove up the block, passing my sister-in-law's house, which was, for now, still standing.

Los Angeles City Fire Department helicopters, hovering low over the neighborhood, continued to make water drops. Fire 3, a 2008 AW139, opened its hatch, and the water that spilled down from it seemed to spray in every direction. By now, the fire had spread to over seven hundred acres.

At 1:36 p.m., as my friend Jake waited on the tarmac at Los Angeles International Airport for his flight back to Washington, his sister, Cara, texted him from Berlin, having watched reports about the Palisades Fire into the late evening.

"Are you still in LA?" she asked. "Should you or someone go grab things from Mom's house???"

"En route back to DC," Jake replied. "Dad and I drove to the desert for this Biden event that was going to be a special thing for him. And then they canceled the whole thing due to dangerously high winds. I decided to get back home. I don't know how to assess the risk to Mom's house, but it seems bad on the face of it. Fire is blowing west, which I think is good news for Palisades village."

"I called Dad to get the update," Cara replied. "He told me that the event was canceled. Going to bed. Love you."

Levine soon took off for DC. As the plane ascended over the Pacific Ocean, he looked out the window to see the Palisades burning.

Gavin Newsom arrived in the Palisades and immediately linked up with Chief Nick Schuler, the deputy director of communications and incident awareness for Cal Fire, the California state firefighting agency. Schuler, who started his career with Cal Fire as a firefighter in San Diego in the late 1990s, worked his way up through the ranks and had seen some of the worst blazes in California history. When he was on the 2003 Cedar Fire, in the Cleveland National Forest, he witnessed an inferno that burned nearly three hundred thousand acres, taking with it the lives of fourteen civilians and one firefighter. He didn't think he would ever experience anything more destructive. In the years since, nine California fires were larger in size.

Just after two in the afternoon, Schuler, who had raced up from San Diego where he still lives, met the governor at the incident command post at Will Rogers Beach for a briefing. From their vantage point at sea level, they could see the Palisades engulfed—but the worst of it was out of sight. Newsom, who said hello to firefighting teams that had been pre-positioned after the National Weather Service alert from Northern California, wanted to see it.

"Hey, Nick, I can't. We can't do any more briefings. Let's go."

"You know, Governor, for us to go any farther—any closer in—you know, it's a pretty challenging situation."

"Well," Newsom responded, "I want to see it."

The men hopped into their vehicles—Newsom in a black SUV, part of a three-vehicle motorcade driven by his California Highway Patrol security detail—and Schuler in his white Chevy Tahoe. They made their way just north of the command post up Surfview Drive to a dead end where the hillside was obscured almost entirely by bright-orange flames and dark smoke just behind homes. Newsom and Schuler got out of their vehicles and surveyed the scene. Embers were raining down. A large, green plastic trash bin—set out for pickup day—was picked up by the winds and hurled across the street.

The governor had visited the sites of countless fires but had never been so close to flames. He felt his eyeballs warming. Recoiling, he jumped back into the car to grab his aviator sunglasses for protection. Newsom, wearing tan lace-up desert boots and a blue sweater with the California state animal, the grizzly bear, on the front and the number forty, representing his governorship, on his left sleeve, stood with his hands in the back pockets of his jeans as he and Schuler watched the fire grow.

The Cal Fire deputy director pointed out how the fire was spreading, gesturing south toward the Palisades Highlands. With sirens blaring and black-and-white squad cars from the Los Angeles County Sheriff's Department on the street, Schuler took off his sunglasses to wipe ash from his eyes, while Newsom, cell phone in hand, shot video of what he was seeing: palm trees igniting and fire spreading to homes.

Within minutes, the situation deteriorated quickly. The fire spread, pushed rapidly by wind gusts that were also making the governor lose his footing. Newsom's normally coiffed salt and pepper hair was blowing in all directions. A massive blast blew through, carrying with it smoke, heat, and more embers, now covering both Schuler and the governor, and causing Schuler to flinch and shove Newsom back toward the car for safety.

"Let's go!" Schuler told the governor, who suddenly felt something land in his hair.

Jesus, Newsom thought, *what the hell is going on here?*

Schuler reflected on all of the times he'd communicated the severity of a fire for the general public, testified in hearings, explained the need for emergency resources—but there was nothing like seeing how, in seconds, Pacific Palisades was exploding. Having spent twenty-seven years in the fire service, he knew what they were looking at—Santa Ana winds breathing extraordinary life into the flames—was going to outpace whatever resources were thrown at the firefight, even blocks from the beach.

NBC News's national broadcast feed was a special report about former president Jimmy Carter's casket being brought to the US Capitol Rotunda, where it would lie in state until the following morning. At around two forty-five in the afternoon, not long before Los Angeles resident Vice President Kamala Harris—whose Brentwood home was a short drive from the Palisades Fire—addressed the assembled dignitaries, including members of the Biden administration, Congress, and justices of the Supreme Court, Los Angeles burned. I joined our streaming network from the courtyard of our studios to explain the images that were coming in, wearing the jean jacket I came to work in and an NBC News hat.

"The Palisades is the neighborhood that I was born and raised in, I grew up in. And to see these pictures, I don't think in my lifetime I've ever seen anything like this.

"What the National Weather Service says is going on is about as bad as it can get in terms of danger from fire in Southern California. Even here at the bureau at Universal Studios, where NBC News is based, we're about twenty miles away from there, and while some of my colleagues are on the ground there, we can feel the winds here. I just saw two of those firefighting aircraft fly overhead heading west out to battle the flames there in the Palisades.

"And we're talking about areas like the Palisades Highlands, where there's maybe as many as a thousand homes. People literally live up in the Santa Monica Mountains. I, for most of my life, lived in the Santa Monica Mountains of Pacific Palisades, and it is a very difficult area to evacuate from in conditions like this."

A gust of wind hit me in the back, and the camera shook.

"There are very limited routes in and out, especially the areas of the Palisades that are up in the Santa Monica Mountains.

"You're looking at pictures of places like Lachman Lane. I grew up two or three blocks away from some of the pictures that you're seeing on the screen. And as I said, this is a very unique, very rare . . ."

A massive gust of wind blew through my live shot position at Universal, across the city from the Palisades. Even from there, the situation felt, as I said live and in the moment, "as dangerous as I think we've seen it, at least in my lifetime in Southern California."

I cleared the live report and went back inside to make final preparations for heading to the Palisades, making a beeline for the bureau chief's office off the newsroom.

"Take the 101 to Malibu," Polly suggested while relaying reports of nightmarish traffic conditions that were developing on the most direct route to my hometown from our office: through the valley, down the Sepulveda Pass, and cut inward toward the coast—either on the Santa Monica Freeway or down Sunset Boulevard. But that was the way I wanted to go, and probably still should, I thought. Before I left, I joined the broadcast once again, twenty-five minutes after my first appearance. It was obvious what was happening.

"Those flames"—now visible in images coming in from our crews on the ground at the corner of the Pacific Coast Highway and Sunset Boulevard, in front of the famous Gladstone's seafood restaurant—"have traveled miles from the places where they started this morning down to, literally, the Pacific Ocean.

"This is a life-threatening situation," I stressed. "Not just for the people in this area but throughout large swaths of Southern California. You do not see winds like this."

I wrapped up at 3:12 p.m. by communicating what I knew:

that Governor Newsom had arrived in Southern California and was about to brief the assembled press. I pulled out my IFB—the earpiece we wear to hear the anchor back in the studio—and popped off my microphone. Back inside, I was handed a bag of company-issued fire gear and tossed the keys to the rental by Julia Lee. Producer Bianca Seward and I started gearing up to head out.

Before we left, the two of us practically raided the self-serve bodega in the basement of the office, knowing we'd likely be spending the night in the car. Directly outside the doors of the snack area sat our white Jeep Wagoneer, waiting for us. We loaded everything we had—the Clif Bars, Coke Zeros, and trail mix, the fire gear and two-way radios and media placards—and set off in a three-car caravan.

The strong winds had toppled power lines in Altadena, on the other side of Los Angeles County in the foothills of the San Gabriel Mountains—one of the areas that Dr. Ariel Cohen and Dave Gomberg at the National Weather Service warned could receive direct hits from the mountain waves that would pour down the face of the San Gabriel Mountains and into the San Gabriel Valley.

Jake Torres, an engineer for the Los Angeles County Fire Department, was driving for its Nineteens, a station in La Cañada Flintridge, home of the Jet Propulsion Laboratory. But they had been pre-positioned in Twelves's first-in: Altadena. Twelves, built in 1928, is the oldest continually operating fire station in Los Angeles County. A single-engine firehouse, its proximity to the San Gabriels means that the company is often called to duty when a brush fire breaks out. The station itself is small, one garage; to its right, an arch hangs over a driveway where the firefighters can park their vehicles.

Torres and his team pulled up to Fair Oaks Avenue and Loma

Alta Drive, a four-way intersection in a residential neighborhood with a bus stop and giant pine trees on three of the corners. The aboveground wires that ran across the intersection were typical for the area, where a thirty-mile-per-hour speed limit was meant to protect the community's children. They got to work securing the downed lines and touching base with Edison, the power company, to take over once they had wrapped up. Torres was working overtime—his third day on the clock. He and probably every other Los Angeles County firefighter not dispatched to the Palisades Fire were wondering when it might happen.

Inside Twelves, less than two miles away, the small crew on duty—including newly promoted Captain Joshua Swaney—were glued to the news, too, unsure if they'd get called out.

"They're going to keep us here because of the wind event," he told his company of what he was hearing from his superiors, especially because of all those utility wires like the ones that Torres and Nineteens were dealing with in his jurisdiction. None of them were below grade, or underground, and the potential for wires-down calls was high. And they just kept coming in.

6

"It Looks Like a War Zone"

IN AN ALTERNATE UNIVERSE, THE DRIVE I WAS MAKING from the San Fernando Valley to Pacific Palisades would be one with a surfboard on top of my car. Not often, but a handful of times, on non-busy days at work, I'd drive in with my "log"—a nine-foot five-inch fiberglass thing of beauty that spends too much time hanging on a rack at my house—strapped to the top of my car. When I had taken care of whatever was on the agenda that day, I'd make my way to the west side to hop in the water. I'm not a good surfer, but I love it.

The forecast for Sunset Point probably looked awful to a more experienced surfer, but a one- to two-foot forecast through early afternoon with a decent tide is my favorite way to surf the spot just south of Gladstone's, whose parking lot is a costly $11 backup to the free parking along PCH. The 1963 classic *Surfing Guide to Southern California*, by Bill Cleary and David H. Stern, describes my home surf spot—currently the incident command post for the Palisades Fire and filling up quickly with journalists arriving on the scene this way:

> Long lines move in past point and develop into slow mushy waves on most all winter and summer swells

> (2–4 feet). But some larger winter swells (4–8 feet) produce good hard-breaking waves; long peak holds up and allows a fast shoot. . . .
>
> Location: 4 miles north of Santa Monica Canyon, just below Sunset Boulevard. Area is part of Will Rogers Beach State Park. Surfing allowed all day. Los Angeles City Lifeguard on duty 10 AM to 6 PM daily in summer. Parking on highway overlooking surf. Expensive yet inferior hamburgers at restaurant 100 yards past point.

The offshore winds hitting the surf spot known simply as "Sunset" today were of a different variety than the ones that would improve the slow, mushy waves I love so much, carrying with them thick black smoke from fires burning at the intersection of Sunset Boulevard and Coast Highway. But I wouldn't see them on the way to the Palisades.

I was excited and nauseated and nervous and scared all at once as we pulled out, but I didn't say anything to Bianca. We got on the freeway and, against the advice of our bureau chief, took (and forgive *The Californians* of *Saturday Night Live* vibe here) the 101 westbound to the 405 southbound and got off at Sunset Boulevard. It was the drive I had made coming home from high school hundreds of times. Bianca and I gossiped about work and recalled stories from the campaign trail, and I assured her I knew where we were going and what I was getting us into.

Would we really be getting on television tonight, she asked? MSNBC was in funeral and political coverage, and the correspondents already deployed to the field would be filing for *NBC Nightly News*, which would be on the air within an hour. I promised her we would. At some point along the journey, I wrote an email to the executives in charge of MSNBC and its primetime coverage: Rashida Jones, Rebecca Kutler, and Greg Kordick.

> Hi guys
>
> LA Fire is in my childhood neighborhood . . . if we break from politics tonight. It's a once in a generation fire here in LA. maybe bigger. Heading that way now will be there overnight with a crew
>
> On cell if you need

As we made our way through traffic, elected officials stepped up to the podium at the command post at Will Rogers Beach to give the latest on the fire—now 1,200 acres "and growing, based on aerial reconnaissance," said Los Angeles Fire Department Chief Kristin Crowley, in a black LAFD cap and yellow Nomex jacket. Evacuation orders were now in place for approximately thirty thousand residents—more than the entire population of the Palisades.

She was flanked by a laundry list of local officials, including Governor Newsom; Los Angeles County Fire Chief Anthony Marrone; Los Angeles County Supervisor Lindsey Horvath; Los Angeles Police Department Chief Jim McDonnell; the local city councilwoman, Traci Park; and the acting mayor of Los Angeles—City Council President Marqueece Harris-Dawson—standing in for the absent *actual* mayor of Los Angeles, Karen Bass. By the start of the press conference, she was en route, via a military flight, back to LA early from her diplomatic mission to Ghana.

"We are not out of danger. The National Weather Service has predicted that the winds are going to pick up and get worse," Chief Marrone said.

Gavin Newsom took the podium.

"Hell of a way to start a new year," he said sardonically before reminding those watching that this fire was the third in a series over the last several months. Both the Franklin Fire in Malibu and the Mountain Fire in Ventura County had been preceded by particularly dangerous situation warnings, like the one that was issued the day before.

"There's no fire season. It's fire year. It's year round," he said.

Newsom, who had visited the fire line an hour before, ran through the pre-positioning of hundreds of personnel and firefighting assets. But he acknowledged in the same breath that "we're not out of the woods by any stretch of the imagination."

The governor, based on the mutual-aid effort underway and a fire that was literally encroaching on the location where he and fellow officials were meeting the press, knew that he wouldn't be going back to Sacramento tonight.

It was now very clear to Eric Mendoza that the fire he and his fellow members of Sixty-Nines believed they had beaten back in the Palisades Highlands had actually blown past them: Structures were burning in his fire station's jurisdiction. And there's nothing more personal to a firefighter than protecting that domain.

That's our area, he thought. *The wind is just nuts.*

Captain Jeff Brown instructed his company to get on the move.

"We need to go. There's something going on over there that we can't see. There's fire in the Palisades."

Mendoza, perched in the bucket of his fire engine, helped guide the massive truck down Palisades Drive. Winding through the canyon to the left, there were choppers dropping water. Fire was jumping from side to side. All alone wearing a headset and steering the back wheels, Mendoza listened to radio traffic and scanned the horizon from his bird's-eye view above the rest of his company.

Whoa. We're going into a war zone. It looks like a war zone. We're burning up.

The scene they came upon at Sunset Boulevard was out of a disaster film. Cars crashing into one another. Cars abandoned. Cars on fire. People running. Power lines starting to drop. The driver swerved through traffic. Around people. Mendoza was whipping the bucket to an extent that even he couldn't believe.

We're at war. This is what war has to look like.

"Hey! We got wires down! Lines down! Post over there you can't see," he told the front of the truck.

Mendoza was heading toward Eric Gonzales, another fireman from Sixty-Nines who had stayed back at the station that morning. When the fire broke out, Gonzales hopped in the plug buggy—a pickup truck—with all his gear and without radio communication. It was a free-for-all. Gonzales had started scouting all of the streets in and around the Palisades village. No water, no nothing. Just a pickup truck. Reaching him by cell phone, Captain Jeff Brown wanted to know what he saw, asking, "Where should we go?"

"El Medio," reported Gonzales. "There's homes up there. No companies." People were trying to put out the fire themselves.

"Let's go," snapped Brown.

Mendoza whipped the rear wheels of the truck along the curves of Sunset Boulevard until on his right-hand side, rising up to the peak of a hilly stretch of the street, he was able to see over the front of the truck and view Palisades Charter High School on his right. Palm trees were on fire. Utility poles were blocking the road. More power lines down. With detritus blanketing the streets, the drive up El Medio and into the residential neighborhood would be next to impossible.

What do we do with this big old thing? he thought.

Looking around, there was only one option.

You know what? Leave it.

Leaving behind a fire engine during a massive blaze is batshit, but circumstances left them no other choice. Mendoza and the rest of the men on the truck parked it on the center median of

Sunset near El Medio to avoid being struck by power lines that may fall. On the north side of Sunset were both the Lutheran Church—where I had my Bar Mitzvah because our temple next door was under construction—and the Presbyterian Church, which is perched on a hillside made to seem even taller because of a giant tower that climbs into the sky, crosses visible on all sides. Across Sunset was Pali High.

The men of Sixty-Nines jumped into the pump truck and left behind the fire engine—still running—not knowing if they'd make it back or whether it would be burned to the ground when they returned. Driving up El Medio, fire was visible as they followed the curves toward the base of the engulfed mountain behind it. A slow rightward bend opens to a straightaway climb and then a sharp left until they saw what Gonzales had called them about.

People, visible through the smoke, protecting their houses with garden hoses. Fire was torching across, wind whipping like Mendoza had never seen. With two other vehicles from Sixty-Nines already on the block, they jumped out and were immediately battered by not only the heat of the flames but also the wind and embers. As they would fly toward Mendoza he would push them away. Hose in hand, he and his team lay flat on their stomachs in the middle of the street, doing whatever they could to protect themselves as they worked to attack the flames.

Eyes burning, and starting to feel dehydrated, he realized that even after doubling up his goggles, they weren't doing the job. Physically, the firemen were fighting. Mentally, they were adjusting. But burning eyes made everything feel impossible—like someone was shoving needles into them. It was unbearably hot, even on the pavement where he lay with his hose opened all the way up. The thoughts that ran through his mind were whipping as hard as the wind.

Are we going to get smoke inhalation? Heat exhaustion? We're going to have to rinse our eyes out for days. I'm going to be coughing up black stuff.

The firefight went on for hours. Home after home burned. The smoke was so thick and the fire so hot, it was impossible by looking around alone to figure out how long the men had been there or what hour it was. Melted metal puddles formed as cars and their components first exploded, then burned, then at last liquefied—a sign that the fire's most intense heat exceeded 1,000 degrees. Eric Mendoza's adrenaline was pumping and his sense of time combusted with the material objects around him. But despite the hell he was living through, Mendoza's attention to the fight would not be diverted. He pushed aside his fears. He did not think about dying.

7

"It Is So Difficult to Breathe"

THE WIND GUSTS COMING OVER THE SANTA MONICA Mountains were approaching seventy miles per hour as the clock struck four in the afternoon. "Explosive" is how meteorologist Dr. Ariel Cohen of the NOAA/National Weather Service described the conditions, which included what is known as a "mountain wave" process. Mountain waves shunt momentum down to the ground, and when they occur as part of a Santa Ana wind event, they can become exceptionally dangerous.

Twenty-four hours before those gusts, on the afternoon of January 6, Dr. Cohen convened an emergency phone call with representatives of the Angeles National Forest, the massive and mountainous protected lands hovering over the Los Angeles Basin mostly in the San Gabriel Mountains. On the call with him was Robert Garcia, the forest's fire chief.

Dr. Cohen's message got their attention:

"We've dealt with red flag warnings," said Dr. Cohen. "This is not a typical red flag warning. This is an all-or-nothing potential mountain-wave event. We're not just talking about Santa Clarita, Porter Ranch, Simi Valley, Moorpark, Camarillo—your normal wind corridor. We're talking about urban parts of Los Angeles County, directly below the forest: Pasadena, Glendora,

Arcadia, Altadena. The front side of the 210 Freeway corridor. The Los Angeles County Basin."

The fire hadn't reached there, so maybe, at least for the foothills of the San Gabriels, it would be the nothing of all-or-nothing. But as the fire ripped through the Palisades, forecasts were calling for gusts in and around the wildland-urban interface at the base of the Angeles National Forest to reach as high as the thirties and forties by late afternoon. By ten o'clock, they'd exceed fifty and continue into the next day.

But the focus remained on the Palisades and nearby observation posts, where the fire was already burning out of control. And because of the ember casts causing fires to flare up far from the battles being fought by the likes of Sixty-Nines, even the incident command post on Pacific Coast Highway was at risk.

On the beach in the Palisades, KNBC's Tracey Leong watched one of those spot fires burn down a trailer park just above the command post, at times apologizing to her audience for gulping for air through her nose and mouth, barely protected by her KN95 mask.

"It is so difficult to breathe. It is so difficult to see."

Minutes later, two adjacent lifeguard towers erupted on Will Rogers Beach, the light-blue wood structures looking like fuel in a campfire, their stilts and pillars consumed by so much heat and flame, so hot, they took on a neon glow. In the winter, they are often moved away from the water to protect the storm surge—but never toward it to protect them from embers of a firestorm.

I called out over the two-way radio the exact coordinates from where I hoped to report live in the heart of the Palisades to cameramen J. B. Rutagarama and Alan Rice—one of whom would be running audio for the reporting we were about to transmit live because all of our NBC personnel had been dispatched to cover the fire. But it became clear we weren't going to get there.

The edges of the village itself were burning, with at least six homes on Radcliffe Avenue, running parallel to Temescal Canyon Road, combusting. One chimney was spewing so much black smoke it was easy to imagine how the house was filled with it. The back side of the home was Haverford Avenue, even closer yet to the heart of the Palisades—supermarkets, restaurants, doctors' offices.

The sounds of fire alarms, crackling homes, and explosions pierced the air at a time when the voices of families heading to an early dinner on the neighborhood's walkable streets would normally be heard.

With twenty-five minutes until the sun would set on Sunset Boulevard, we stopped short of where I wanted to land. We were in the Palisades Riviera, a stretch of multimillion-dollar homes on both sides of the street, and directly in front of us was no longer a sky full of smoke but the entire ridge of Will Rogers State Historic Park spewing dark-orange flames, the smoke we had seen on approach rising directly from them. Going all the way into the village wasn't a good idea—and here we had a vantage point that allowed us to see the fire without inhaling the smoke and ash that was blowing in the direction of where I had wanted to stop.

We pulled over on the shoulder, and I got out of our Wagoneer, throwing on my yellow Nomex jacket and an NBC News hat. It was a quarter to five. We called into the control room in New York and were patched into the broadcast winding down on our streaming network, NBC News NOW. I put an AirPod in my left ear and dialed on my cell phone the number I was given to hear Tom Llamas, the anchor in New York. Between us and the burning flames, I saw a man in a red baseball cap standing in front of a white Tesla Model 3 and speaking into a cell phone. An elderly woman and a dog sat in the car, watching the fire burn closer. A huge yucca tree, despite its rigidity, swayed with each shift of the wind.

I stood ready to join the broadcast, looking directly into the camera being operated by Rice, hoisted on his right shoulder with a backpack in which was a device that allows us to transmit live. Before I knew it, I heard Llamas's voice introducing me as I watched my neighborhood burn.

"One of our teams is right by the fire tonight. Jacob Soboroff is live on the scene for us. Sunset Boulevard in Pacific Palisades."

The camera cut to me, holding what we call the stick microphone in my right hand, eyes squinting to protect them from the wind, the white Tesla visible over my left shoulder as the fire poured from the hillside.

"Jacob, talk to me about what you're seeing out there."

"Tom, this is an—I have to tell you, this is the neighborhood I was born and raised in. I've never seen anything like this in my entire life. I'm standing on the corner of Sunset Boulevard and Amalfi Drive in the Pacific Palisades part of Los Angeles. You can see the fire over on the ridge there as it approaches Will Rogers Park. On the other side of that mountain you're looking at—these are the Santa Monica Mountains as the hill goes up in flames as I'm speaking to you right now—is the Pacific Palisades village. Beyond the Pacific Palisades village are the Pacific Palisades Highlands, where we have been watching all day as literally thousands of people are evacuating from up in the hills."

As I spoke, the man in the red baseball cap walked out into the middle of the street to check on the fire's progress; after catching a glimpse, he hurried back toward his car.

"It has been a complete gridlock here on the west side of Los Angeles." The fire, I told Llamas, was "as big as I have seen in my lifetime."

As I reported in real time, I walked over to the man watching the fire.

"Sir, we're live on NBC News. Do you mind if I get a quick word with you?"

"Sure."

"What's your name?"

"My name's Nick."

"Nick, Jacob. It's nice to meet you, and I'm sorry it's under this circumstance."

When I got up close to him, I could see he was wearing dark plastic-rimmed glasses and had a mustache and goatee. He told me he was standing in front of his home.

"First thing this morning, when the first truck came by, I knew there was something going on," he recounted. "And I knew when it was in the Highlands, in the bottleneck, it was going to be a problem—and then it was."

The bamboo shoots behind him were dancing in all directions.

He told me he had lived in the Palisades for five years, and we walked together to get a better view of the fire's proximity to his home.

"What's your calculation? When are you going to go?" I asked him.

"I've been watching it all day," he explained. "Once the cloud plume is close to getting to be over our heads—which is about right now—I'm out of here. But right now, I'm trying to stay as long as I can. My mom's fortune went into purchasing this home."

He pointed to the car, and it became clear to me that there were multiple dogs inside, sitting in the front because the back seat was jammed with boxes and whatever else he'd loaded up to get ready to evacuate.

"This is all we got, and I'm going to try and stay as long as I can."

"What's stopping you from leaving? We can feel the wind coming this direction right now."

"Just fucking hope? I don't know," Nick replied as he stared into the distance at the approaching flames. "I've been watching the air drops all day."

I thanked Nick and sent him on his way to get ready to evacuate, and looked back into the camera as the wind blew my hair from back to front so that it looked like the palm trees being tossed around behind me. Then another gust whipped my hair back in the opposite direction.

"Hey, Jacob?" Llamas interrupted. "You said you've never seen anything like it. What's the difference? Is it the wind there tonight?"

"It's not only the wind event—this is a once-in-a-lifetime [wind event] combined with the dryness. We have barely had any rain here in Los Angeles throughout the winter season. A negligible amount. I don't think it's been enough to really even measure. And so the combination of all of the vegetation that's grown with the last couple of years of rain that we've had here, combined with the dryness right now, is a catastrophic sort of condition for a fire like this to break out, especially in such a populated area here on the west side of LA.

"We've talked about fires before. There was a fire at Pepperdine University out in Malibu just a couple of weeks if not a month ago, but certainly not in a place where tens of thousands of people live, like this."

With that, I signed off and looked at my phone. In our family group chat was a text from my brother, imploring my sisters to evacuate their homes on the west side.

> Not alarmist but make a plan. Started as nothing. Now it's going all the way to the ocean. We may lose our home. Just stay one step ahead and safe most important please !!

> Guys don't be silly nothing is for sure. They're expecting mega winds all night. It could take one ember to move the whole thing miles away. Just make a plan.

I let them know I had made it to the Palisades and that I would be coming up soon on MSNBC. At the moment the sun set behind the mountain ridge in the distance, the fire's orange glow illuminated the smoke clouds above it; they seemed to tower ever higher over the rapidly darkening streetscape in front of me. I snapped a photo and sent it to the thread.

"Will Rogers Park engulfed."

8

"If He's Staying, I'm Staying"

THE THOUSANDS OF GALLONS OF WATER BEING DROPPED from helicopters and fixed-wing aircraft that my interviewee Nick had watched from the corner of Amalfi and Sunset had been falling since the start of the Palisades Fire that morning. By the time I encountered him on Sunset, even more resources were on the way. As the sun went down, chief pilot Dan Child of the Los Angeles Fire Department took off from Van Nuys Airport, relieving a fellow pilot who had been flying over the Palisades Fire most of the day. Wind was sustained around thirty-five knots—a high risk level for flying, but so is fighting fires from a helicopter. That's the job.

Not all of the choppers have a wind limit, but LAFD Air Operations does maintain a limit of forty knots in the mountains—where flying is more turbulent—and a fifty-knot limit within the city environment. Even with increasing wind in the forecast, so long as Child and Air Ops could be effective, they would continue to try to do as much as they could.

Over the Palisades, Child's aircraft hovered at a higher altitude than the copters under his command. The sixteen-year Air Ops veteran directed operations in a command-and-control role, providing feedback to the pilots below. HLCO—helicopter coordinator—is the name of the gig. All pilots for the Los Angeles Fire Department were once firefighters on the line. While many spent years beating back blazes on the ground, it is a separate skill set entirely from putting out fires from the sky—a literal high-wire act that requires split-second decisions about altitude, airspeed, which doors to open and the volume of water to drop, and, of course, the wind.

How fast am I going? How high am I above the ground? How many doors do I have open? What is the wind doing? What direction am I coming from? Is this an uphill drop? Downhill? How effective can I be? All these questions and more race through the minds of Dan Child and the other airborne firefighters. What he was seeing was that the water was spraying everywhere, no matter the target.

"Hey, you need to offset—the wind really carried that one," he instructed one pilot. "Offset three rotor diameters to your right."

"OK, copy that."

Frustration was building, though, as the wind's speed and direction would shift on a dime, and pilots were having difficulty holding altitude.

"I'm losing about a thousand to two thousand feet of altitude just in a turn," radioed one of the pilots under Child's command. "What is going on over here?"

Down drafts from the mountain were blowing on either side—forces combining to push the choppers around with "downers"—the strong winds that were causing the altitude drops. With choppers needing to descend at times to just fifty to a hundred feet off the ground, the danger was increasingly evident. Over the radio, a chopper sent word about the difficulties they were facing.

"We're getting—our wind report currently is sixty-nine miles an hour, gusting to eighty-nine."

As chief pilot, Child knew that none of his pilots would pack it in unless he made the call—they would never suggest turning back, the rationale being *If he's staying, I'm staying.*

Down on terra firma, the air cover was a welcome sight to the men of Twenty-Threes—who had stayed, too. Tim Larson, up in the first-in of his station, had been told as a young firefighter that the veterans would regale them with tales about windy days when you'd open your hose line and water would shoot ten feet out of the line, then spray in whichever direction the wind was blowing. That's exactly what was happening. The dozen or so engines up in the Highlands with them were doing everything they could. But Larson, the engineer on a pump truck, was watching his vehicle's fuel slowly run out.

"Jacob, it looks really bad there. How's it going?"

That was the introduction I got at 5:31 p.m. local time, 8:31 p.m. eastern, from my colleague and friend Chris Hayes on MSNBC. Chris and I have covered many consequential live events together—but never one in my childhood neighborhood. Although the sun had fully set and darkness had set in, the sky behind me looked like someone had snapped an orange glow stick and held it atop the horizon.

I wasn't supposed to appear on Chris's show for another twenty minutes. But I called the control room and made the case to his producer, Tina Cone, that what we were seeing was urgent and that—honestly—I had no idea if the flames would hold off for that long. I could hear Tina talking to others in the control room at 30 Rock. She came back on the line and told me to stand by—that after a segment about President-elect Trump losing a bid to halt his sentencing in his hush money case and the subsequent commercial break, I'd be up next. Thirty-one minutes after the hour, I heard Chris set me up and ask me to explain what I was seeing.

"It's awful, Chris. Pacific Palisades is the neighborhood I was born and raised in. About twenty-three thousand people live in this neighborhood. It's a coastal community in the City of Los Angeles and much of Pacific Palisades is on fire as I speak to you tonight. What you're looking at over my shoulder is the ridge of Will Rogers State Historic Park. It's a big, beautiful park in between where I'm standing right now and what's called the Palisades Riviera and the Palisades village. The center of town. Where thousands of people congregate on a daily basis.

"This fire started in an area that's known . . . as the Palisades Highlands. And that's an area where there's maybe five hundred or a thousand homes, and it's very, very dangerous in a situation like this. One road or two roads in, and there's only one or two roads out."

The wind started whipping my hair so hard that it was hitting me in my left eye. I kept pushing it back.

"There has been gridlock on these streets much of the day here because of how dry it has been—how little rain we have gotten over the course of the last several months. A wind event like this is not one we see often in Southern California. These Santa Ana winds come in, and they blow over the mountains toward the coast, and it is like a tinderbox out here. And it's not a wildfire out in the wilderness. This is in the middle of an urban part of the City of Los Angeles, where, as I mentioned, tens of thousands of people live and are currently evacuating from as I speak to you tonight, Chris."

Just then a police cruiser arrived on the scene to block people from venturing any farther than we were positioned. Its flashing lights illuminated the darkness behind me, revealing the silhouettes of four people standing there, listening to my report for any update or news they could glean.

"It is an LAPD tactical alert," I went on. "Which means all

LAPD officers are on duty tonight because this is an event unlike one we have seen in recent times here in Los Angeles, Chris."

"That looks really bad," he sympathized, "and I hope that you and everyone there can stay safe. Jacob, thank you very much."

"Thanks, Chris."

At 5:33 p.m., I cleared MSNBC and over the next four and a half minutes Bianca, J.B., and Alan made the technical adjustments to get me lined up with our streaming network to talk to a colleague of mine from the Los Angeles bureau, Gadi Schwartz, on his program. I had spotted Gadi as I was walking out the door from that live position in our courtyard at Universal.

"Man, I just saw you at the bureau here a little while ago," Gadi said.

The sky behind me was moving from a dark shade of orange to almost yellow—the jacket I was wearing matched it almost exactly. And I explained to Gadi much of what I had just told Chris. But as I stood there, details about my childhood started to bubble up in my brain, as if they were boiling to the surface as the intensity of the flames increased.

"I went to school just down this way," I said, pointing away from the Palisades village and toward Brentwood. Then I turned and pointed toward the village. "My house was on the other side of that ridge that me and my four siblings came of age in." My voice cracked ever so slightly. Every time I turned and looked over my shoulder, I could only guess what was happening on the other side of the state park that was now just an inferno.

All of my memories were sort of sticking together like a ball of putty I needed to pull apart, including details about the three houses my parents, four siblings, and I had called home in different pockets of the Palisades.

"The Palisades is a wonderful community," I told Gadi. What else could I say? I was trying to manifest that it was still actually there, over the raging inferno behind me. I feared it wasn't and was unsure of what the next few minutes—forget about hours—would bring. "It is a vibrant part of the City of Los Angeles, and, unlike some of these wildfires we've seen in the past—and I don't want to minimize it; *of course* we have seen casualties and we have seem homes burn—this is a massive wildfire in an urban setting. It's in the City of Los Angeles in a place where there are thousands and thousands of homes.

"Here at the corner of Amalfi Drive and Sunset Boulevard you continue to see cars come around that bend"—the infamous Dead Man's Curve we didn't even make it to on our way in—"and then turn right around and come out because, as I said, much of Pacific Palisades, California, tonight, in the heart of the City of Los Angeles, is on fire, Gadi."

"I'm so sorry, Jacob, for what you're going through, because this is where you grew up. And I hate to ask because you said your childhood home is . . . and then you pointed in the direction of the flames . . .

"Do you know how your home is?"

"I think when the sun comes up tomorrow morning—after the winds continue to get more and more intense tonight, there's going to be a lot of damage for all of us to survey. I've got family members tonight that evacuated just like thousands of people here."

As if on cue, two fire engines rolled past, from Eighty-Eights in Sherman Oaks and Ninety-Twos in Century City, swinging around the bend toward Dead Man's Curve and into the heart of the fire to find out answers to those questions before I could. Gadi had the same thought that so many of the firefighters were worried about at that very moment:

"All of Southern California right now, at least a very large part of it, is in the direct line of these Santa Ana winds, so just praying that nothing happens elsewhere."

"I can't stress enough—and I have a text thread going with my own family—how important it is to get out right now if you live in or around these areas," I said. "It is time to get out if you haven't left yet."

As I was talking to Gadi, above the outdoor swimming pool at Pali High, the stadium lights were illuminated as they always were at this time of night. But the school's fire alarm was blaring. Embers were blowing horizontally across the landscape, ash creating a black layer across the top of the water.

Still, the thirteen-lane, thirty-meter pool, named the Maggie Gilbert Aquatic Center, was faring well relative to the homes across Temescal Canyon that were virtually all burned to the ground less than an hour earlier.

Firefighters rolled by: Twentys from Echo Park, near where I live now, by Dodger Stadium; Elevens from Westlake–MacArthur Park; Threes from Bunker Hill in downtown Los Angeles—all over twenty miles from their first-ins. Complete chaos. Darsha Philips of KNBC was there, reporting live.

"When these wind gusts come through, it is so intense, and when it hits that fire and that flame, it is like a blowtorch."

Colleen Williams was in the anchor chair. Part of my core memories of growing up in the Palisades was watching her and her colleagues deliver the local news. She raised a pertinent question about the water supply.

"When you talk about how all of the Palisades has been evacuated and all the firefighters out there. When you look back and see how they are trying to protect this school, does there appear to be a problem with water supply at all?"

"We are not hearing or seeing any water drops," Philips replied. "And we actually haven't seen firefighters trying to douse the area with water. And I do not know what the water supply situation is at this time."

Tim Larson of Twenty-Threes and Captain Dan Child of Air Ops had some awareness regarding the water-availability issue. Both men were already worried about their ability to put water on the flames.

The men of Ninety-Fours were posted up on Tellem Drive, around the corner from where my brother and pregnant sister-in-law had evacuated seven hours earlier. Things weren't looking good. The winds continued to shift, and from a perch above them on Vista Grande, looking down into the canyon, all that was visible was a radiant red. The lights of Ninety-Fours illuminated the hillside between them, as embers rained down.

At almost exactly the same moment, on MSNBC, Chris Hayes was showing some of Vice President Harris's remarks at the memorial for the late president Jimmy Carter, lying in state at the US Capitol. As she ticked through his accomplishments, and her hometown burned thousands of miles away, a signature initiative of the Carter administration seemed especially relevant given what Los Angeles was currently facing.

"Jimmy Carter was a forward-looking president with a vision for the future," she said. "His creation of FEMA, in 1979, which enabled our nation to mobilize a national response to disasters which has helped countless communities rebuild and recover." The Federal Emergency Management Agency would undoubtedly be called to duty in the wake of what was happening in Los Angeles.

Immediately out of that sound bite, Chris Hayes turned back with the short amount of time he had left to bring me back into the broadcast. What Kamala Harris had just highlighted from

President Carter's legacy would be so incredibly critical in what was to come—but there was no way to digest and process it in the moment.

"It's horrible, Chris." The wind was blowing southwesterly in our direction, from behind the engulfed Will Rogers State Historic Park, putting hundreds of homes in the fire's direct path.

"Is there any sense of ETA on containment?"

"Until the winds die down, until we get the marine layer that often sits over this portion of Los Angeles, I don't see a situation—and the meteorologists, firefighters, the other experts—don't see a situation where this gets any better any time in the near future."

Seven minutes later, the first embers drifted down on our location, which I reported live to Alex Wagner on MSNBC. Seventy-Ones raced onto the scene as a 2016 Ram 4500 truck reconfigured as Rescue Ambulance 71 whizzed past with lights flashing and sirens blaring, making its way from LA's Bel Air neighborhood—home to the devastating 1961 Bel Air Fire—ripping around the corner and into the heat of the blaze.

"Never in my lifetime can I remember standing in Pacific Palisades and having the entire community evacuated," I told Alex. "Tomorrow morning is going to be a bleak scene here, and we haven't even seen the beginning of it."

Alex asked about what it felt like to be in Los Angeles, noting, "We're hearing reports of absolute chaos."

"People are going as far as they can as fast as they can away from this part of town," I explained. "When you heard about the scenes earlier today that resulted in those cars being abandoned on the roads, it's because of the development created in places like the Palisades Highlands or at the top of streets like Bienveneda where I lived as a young guy growing up here in Los Angeles. There are very few ways out. There are fire roads, but those fire roads, too, become gridlocked or sometimes impassable.

And so what people did at the beginning of this firestorm"—it was the first time the word entered my thoughts and came out of my mouth—"and I think that's the only way to describe it, is to get out of their cars in places like Sunset Boulevard, places like Kehillat Israel Temple in the middle of Pacific Palisades, and just start walking, because it's a terrifying sight to behold. To stand here and to watch this—I don't quite have the words to describe to you what it's like to be standing here in this part."

What I couldn't put into words then was the sheer scale of what was unfolding around me. It felt as though a tropical storm or hurricane was blowing through our coastal California community, with scalding embers playing the part of pelting rain. The well-manicured lawns of the homes along Sunset Boulevard were being ripped apart and tossed in every direction. Trash cans littering the street were projectiles to be avoided. Residents who had stayed behind were desperate for information. Fear was being transmitted by osmosis and seeping into my skin. Nobody knew what would happen next. If what they were smelling was their lives on fire. And through it, my colleagues and I had to continue to work.

At 6:11 p.m., I cleared Alex's MSNBC broadcast and returned to our rented Wagoneer. Bianca and I hunkered down to collect ourselves before going back on the air in the next hour. At almost the exact same time, forty-five miles away in the foothills of the San Gabriel Mountains above the unincorporated Los Angeles County town of Altadena, the nightmare scenario that Dr. Ariel Cohen and Dave Gomberg of the National Weather Service had warned of came true.

9

"The Perfect Storm"

AROUND 6:10 P.M., AS BLASTING WINDS RUSHED DOWN the southern slopes of the San Gabriel Mountains, power flickered in homes near Eaton Canyon Park, a gateway into the rugged foothills of the Angeles National Forest. Eaton Canyon is an easily accessible respite above Altadena and the other suburban communities that sit on the far-northern end of the San Gabriel Valley. In Eaton Canyon, gently sloping trails lead to a waterfall tucked away in the forest.

For hikers and residents, the steel lattice towers rising from the horizon carrying high-voltage transmission lines up and over the mountains are as recognizable as the bucolic dirt paths, scraggly chapparal, and, at slightly higher elevations, old oaks.

One such power line, the century-old Mesa-Sylmar, owned by SoCal Edison, had been idle for some fifty years. But, as one leading theory under investigation would have it, as seventy-mile-per-hour gusts whipped neighboring active lines, a powerful magnetic current transferred electricity to the dormant line, inducing a spark that set vegetation at the bottom of the tower in Eaton Canyon aflame.

What at first appeared to some Altadenans as merely a campfire-sized flame spread quickly, consuming the base of the tower and then everything around it.

Altadena resident Cate Heneghan, who lived on McNally Avenue, located about two miles west of the ignition, lost power in her home. But there was no visible sign of flames or smoke. Only word of what was happening across the county, in the Palisades. Heneghan, a senior engineer for more than three decades at NASA's Jet Propulsion Laboratory, fired up her small back-up battery to power her laptop and cell phone without realizing the Eaton Fire had begun.

With darkness having fallen, the slopes of Eaton Canyon would rapidly ignite, winds spreading the bright-orange flames, smoke, and embers across the hills and into the neighborhood below.

Robert Garcia, a thirty-year veteran of the US Forest Service and now fire chief for the Angeles National Forest, was sitting in his situation room in Arcadia, a city in the San Gabriel Valley in the shadow of the sprawling forest. He had sent resources and assets to the Palisades to assist in the mutual-aid effort underway to save life and property as the predicted mountain-wave winds cascaded down the Santa Monica Mountains and into the beach-adjacent enclave. On three flat-screens backlit by giant windows, he monitored local news coverage of the Palisades Fire on the left, a network of woodland cameras that are part of the ALERT-California network run by the University of California San Diego, on the center monitor, and on the right, a map of Angeles National Forest.

Wrapping up a coordination call with other agencies, he was discussing what conditions would trigger a total recall of personnel—a balance of bringing on additional staffing but also maintaining a marathon pace, as he calls it, if word came through that fire had broken out in his jurisdiction. Shortly after six o'clock, the first calls rolled in, followed quickly thereafter by many more.

Minutes away from his position in Arcadia, reports indicated a fire had started in approximately the same place where, in 1993, another fire had brought about catastrophic consequences. The Kinneloa Fire began as an out-of-control campfire that feasted on perilously dry brush and ended up destroying nearly two hundred homes—making it one of the worst fires in California history at the time. The damage was largely contained to what firefighters call a wildland-urban interface fire, not a larger conflagration like the one developing in the Palisades. But Garcia knew—and he and his counterparts had been discussing—what an ignition in that part of Los Angeles County would mean under the particularly dangerous situation warning twenty-eight years after the Kinneloa Fire.

"This is what we are going to see more and more frequently," Karen Terrill, a former spokeswoman for the California Department of Foresty and Fire Protection, said to *The New York Times* in 1993.

In the years since, Mother Nature had done anything but settle down. The Kinneloa Fire dropped off the list of California's most destructive fires entirely, as larger and more ferocious blazes consumed the state year after year. And that's why the area remained a major concern for Garcia.

Now it was happening again. Based purely on the location of the reports coming in, the fire chief knew he had a problem.

"Oh, man," he said.

Immediately, he got on the phone with his counterparts from other local fire agencies: Chad Augustin, chief of the Pasadena Fire Department; Brent Bartlett, chief of the Sierra Madre Fire Department; and Anthony Marrone of the LA County Fire Department. Marrone was already at the command post in the Palisades, which was now threatening entire neighborhoods and the largest protected landscape in the Los Angeles region.

Do we have enough personnel to make an effective attack? Garcia pondered.

At 6:26 p.m., in a post on X, Los Angeles City Fire Chief Kristin Crowley recalled all available members to return to duty to a fire that was now consuming more than 2,900 acres:

> All #LAFD members currently off-duty are to call the DOC 213-576-8962 with their availability for recall. #palisadesfire

In Arcadia, Garcia got in his vehicle and raced through the darkness to a command post being established near Eaton Canyon even as firefighters faced a frontal assault of wildfire coming at them. Garcia would reflect later that upon assessing the situation, he realized immediately, "This was one of those worst-case scenarios, for sure."

Also dispatched to the Eaton Fire were Los Angeles County's Nineteens, with Jake Torres driving the engine, and Twelves, with Captain Joshua Swaney. Twelves was on a tree-down call: A massive oak around Lincoln Avenue had crumpled a home when the call for a brush fire in Sixty-Sixes's first-in came through. With no lives in immediate danger and other personnel on the scene, within a minute they were driving, firefighter Gunner Alves in the back seat as they started rolling. Up on the hill they could see the header—the smoke plume coming from Eaton Canyon—and they knew it was going to be a big one.

"Wow, this is a real fire," Alves remarked.

Twelves went to the left flank of the fire, which was encroaching on homes off Altadena Drive alongside Eaton Canyon. Nineteens went to the right flank, near where the Kinneloa Fire had ravaged that neighborhood in 1993. Twelves hooked up to a hydrant, and Alves grabbed a chainsaw off the rig to trim some of the trees along the houses as the fire backed down the hill toward them.

And then it hit, setting off a game of Whac-A-Mole, with little fires becoming bigger fires becoming structure fires all around them.

For Nineteens, instead of the normal staging process for engines to report to the incident commander, they dove right in, adhering to an acronym they learned as probationary firefighters: TIER—take initiative, engage, and report. Houses were burning, and with the power out across so much of Altadena, fire was the only source of light.

Meanwhile, in the Palisades, the scene was downright apocalyptic. The fire had grown with such force, and the winds were so strong, it was hard to make sense of the chaos. Palm trees kept incinerating, and the fire seemed to be falling like rain.

At the command post along Will Rogers Beach, it was impossible to fix a map of the firefight area to the side of one of the vehicles stationed there. The Los Angeles Fire Department made the decision to physically move the command post down Pacific Coast Highway and away from the Palisades because the inferno threatened to overtake their location. Captain Erik Scott, the department spokesman, couldn't stop coughing from the whirling sand, smoke, and ash as he tried to give a public update.

"This is one of the worst wind-driven fires I've had the privilege of being on," he said during a live interview with KNBC, "and I'm even on a type 1 federal incident management team that goes all over the place."

In terms of resources, Scott issued a dire warning about other areas at risk:

"I'll be candid. Your Los Angeles City Fire Department needs more firefighters. We recently did an independent study called the standards of cover, and the statistics showed that due to how fast Los Angeles is expanding that we absolutely do need additional boots on the ground." The captain then called for additional funding, even in the midst of the ongoing emergency, saying, "We're doing the best with what we've got.

"We're dealing with new normals. These wildfires are increasing in severity and duration. We say we're no longer dealing with a fire season. It's year round. And if anybody is in these areas, you don't have to wait until we tell you to go to go."

McNally Avenue in Altadena is one of the namesakes of Rand McNally & Company cofounder Andrew McNally, the Northern Ireland native who had owned much of the land in modern-day Altadena, which he purchased in 1888, according to the *Long Beach Press-Telegram*. The paper reported that before his move to Los Angeles, McNally had settled in Chicago in the mid 1800s and entered the printing business.

Eventually McNally and his partners bought the *Chicago Tribune* print shop and, during the Great Chicago Fire of 1871, one of the largest urban conflagrations in American history, they managed to save two of their printing presses by burying them in sand. (The Great Chicago Fire occurred on the same day as another historic blaze, the Peshtigo Fire in northwest Wisconsin, the deadliest fire in US history, which killed between 1,500 and 2,000.)

McNally's Los Angeles home was at the corner of modern-day Mariposa Street and Santa Rosa Avenue. More than a hundred years later, the Andrew McNally House was added to the National Register of Historic Places on my birthday, March 27, in 2007. The State of California's brief history of the house told the story of its importance to the community:

> The Andrew McNally House is a two-story house designed in the Queen Ann, Shingle style by master architect Frederick L. Roehrig. The house was constructed in 1888, and in 1894 the one-and-a-half-story Smoking Room was added to the southeast corner of the house. . . . The property was listed at the local level of significance in the area of settlement between the years 1888 and 1904, for its association with Andrew McNally. McNally was an early promoter of residential growth in Altadena. His house was the first substantial home built along "Millionaire's Row." McNally's enthusiastic endorsement of Altadena and its agrarian and esthetic charms led wealthy families from the Midwest and East to [build] their winter homes in Altadena.

McNally Avenue was about a mile from the McNally House. And beginning in "the wee hours of Tuesday morning," January 7, Cate Heneghan heard the winds howling, she told me. She hadn't slept well the night before in her small Spanish-style home, an orange front door flanked by windows on both sides and two awnings hanging overhead. Terra-cotta tiles lined the home's roof perimeter, the house set back from the street, separated by native vegetation and a thin concrete walking path to her front door.

As most in Los Angeles County focused their attention on what was happening in the Palisades, over forty miles away, Heneghan had charged her camping lantern, headlamps, phones, and computers, all of which came in handy after McNally Avenue lost power. At 6:56 p.m., from a camera perched atop Mount Wilson, nearly six thousand feet above the Los Angeles Basin, itself tilting side to side in the gusts, a flash was visible adjacent to the orange smoke plume rising from the depths of Eaton Canyon.

Heneghan's text messages soon started to light up with neighbors confirming the worst: A massive fire had broken out in Eaton Canyon. The Los Angeles County Fire Department estimated the fire initially at twenty acres—with the ability to grow to five hundred acres "quickly." Its public information officer, Captain Sheila Kelliher, who was positioned at the Palisades Fire, summed it up succinctly:

"This is the perfect storm, right? We haven't had rain, significant rain, in the last three years—last eight months for sure. These are the most extreme wind conditions we've seen in a decade. And you combine that with low relative humidity . . . and our low fuel moisture, and you put it in somewhere like Eaton Canyon, where the topography just breeds more wind and more weather, it's just the worst-case scenario, to be honest."

For now, Cate Heneghan, with her power out and devices charged, decided to stay put on McNally Avenue, west of the fire, believing it was headed east.

As the clock approached seven in the evening, tenders—trucks carrying thousands of gallons of water—were being rushed into the Palisades. Pressure was dropping in the mountains as the firefighters opened their hoses full-bore. Eric Mendoza and Sixty-Nines, who had abandoned their fire truck on Sunset Boulevard in front of Pali High, started seeing pressures fluctuate from low pressure to no pressure at the top of El Medio.

Up and down. Up and down.

They were shutting down the rigs that did make it up the hill so that water pressure could build back up, then start them up again.

A similar scene was playing out with Tim Larson and the men of Twenty-Threes, who remained in the cul-de-sac of Calle Victoria in the Highlands. He was approached by an older woman who told him, "I've had a rough year. I lost my husband."

There's no way we can lose her house, Larson thought.

"Ma'am, I'm not going to die, but I'm going to freaking just about die saving your house."

As a young man, he'd signed up for a job where he would solve other people's problems, and as conditions far surpassed anything he had ever seen—whether as a hotshot on a Forest Service crew or as the engineer at Twenty-Threes in the Palisades—he committed himself to doing exactly that.

He was still trying to beat back the fire in the part of the Palisades Highlands that had first reported it, but the firestorm's heat, wind, and embers were all beating down on him. He would not allow himself to believe that it could get any worse—that the Palisades as he knew it might be gone. As the fuel in his engine was running precariously low, he would soon be forced to find out.

Inside the Jet Propulsion Laboratory in La Cañada Flintridge, a Mars-on-Earth simulator was used in 2014 to test NASA's Ingenuity Helicopter before it made history flying on the Red Planet in 2021. Atop the same facility, ten miles to the west of Eaton Canyon, both in the foothills of the massive San Gabriel Mountains, sits an emergency helicopter landing pad that was empty when the Eaton Fire began to scream down the canyon and toward Altadena. As winds on this part of Earth approached sixty miles per hour—the speed of a Mars dust storm—veteran Los Angeles news chopper pilot Larry Welk sat atop the JPL helipad looking for water drops. He and the other news choppers in Los Angeles were grounded not because of the wind conditions but because of temporary flight restrictions in place due to President Biden's visit to Los Angeles. POTUS was currently holed up in his Century City hotel, watching the devastation unfold.

For Welk's part, he continued to witness explosions of high-voltage electrical transmission lines, many of which ran through the San Gabriel Mountains in the direct path of the fire. He knew the blaze was much bigger than the twenty acres being reported publicly, and that the water-dropping aircraft would soon face prohibitive conditions that could prevent safe and accurate operations—or worse yet, cause one of them to crash.

Welk had witnessed the beginning of the Palisades Fire in the morning, and it was clear to him that the amount of fire-illuminated smoke he was now seeing, even through the darkness, was as much as he had seen across the county.

10

"We Need to Get to a Better Location"

US FOREST SERVICE FIRE CHIEF ROBERT GARCIA HAD raced from the craftsman-style headquarters of the Angeles National Forest, in Arcadia, to the makeshift incident command post for the Eaton Fire. The fifteen-minute drive to the northwest was directly toward the engulfed mountainside. At the command post, he spoke with Chad Augustin, the fire chief for neighboring Pasadena.

"We need a long-term large command post location," Garcia told him, sharing, as the fire exploded in front of them, that working out of the back of a pickup truck with the fire almost certainly going to overtake them was, obviously, unsustainable.

With multiple jurisdictions already responding—Pasadena police and fire; Los Angeles County sheriff and fire, which were both already at the Palisades Fire forty miles away; his own firefighters from the US Forest Service's Angeles National Forest branch; and Sierra Madre police and fire, which were en route—Garcia's priority was, with the leadership on the scene, to make sure that the Incident Command System was fully operational.

The ICS, a predetermined structure for coordinating a multijurisdictional command-and-control response to wildfires, was pioneered in Southern California in the 1970s after a series of devastating fires, along with the support of Congress. In the 1980s it was adopted by firefighters nationwide, then by the US Coast Guard, which often worked with other agencies in emergency responses. Following the September 11, 2001, terrorist attacks on New York, Pennsylvania, and the Pentagon in the nation's capital, President George W. Bush, through presidential directive, created the National Incident Management System, now used to manage domestic mass casualty incidents of all kinds.

The area around the Eaton Canyon Nature Center, a beautiful facility built in 1998, was no place for an incident command post or for running an ICS. I had been there to drop off my son for his outdoors camp in late July. The camp sent us this report about their excursion on a day of 90-degree heat:

> Our day started with a spectacular find! A baby garter snake was spotted swimming against the current of the stream. . . .
>
> Through the trees and up the valley we went, following along the river until we reached Eaton Canyon's grand waterfall. The kids were so excited to start splashing and run through the cascading waters. Here we took a moment to catch frogs, craft with stones and grass, and sit under the fig trees to enjoy the earthy aroma of their leaves baking in the sun. A perfect water day!

When I picked him up at the end of the day, I ran inside the 7,600-square-foot building that was used to educate visitors about the local wildlife, habitat, and dangers—including fire. The Fire Ecology Trail, and the original Nature Center itself, burned in the 1993 Kinneloa Fire. Visible on it are plants from the "Coastal Sage Scrub plant community," as the Nature Center Association describes them, below the chaparral in the mountains above it. Coffeeberry, scale broom, laurel sumac, Western sycamore, golden currant, mule fat, and more lined the way. But now all that biodiversity was kindling for what Garcia and the other incident commanders were staring at from the back of a pickup truck.

This is like treating patients in an emergency room and having to move them at the same time, he thought.

"We need to get to a better location," he said.

The ICS picked Farnsworth Park, three and a half miles to the northwest.

"That's probably not far enough," Garcia said. But they relocated there anyway.

I was focused so narrowly on the inferno in the Palisades that the severity of the situation in Altadena didn't even come close to registering as I joined Lawrence O'Donnell on MSNBC around seven thirty. I hadn't heard any of the local reports, and we hadn't reported anything about the details of what was playing out ten miles closer to my house and where my wife and kids were than the Palisades Fire. *It can't be as bad as what we're seeing here.*

Lawrence, like me, knew the Palisades well. I had run into him before in the neighborhood when out to dinner with my family and understood that what he was watching was as familiar to him as it was to me. Officers from the Los Angeles Police Department, some wearing masks to protect their lungs from the smoke, had started turning people around by shining flashlights at approaching vehicles as they attempted to go any farther than where we were broadcasting from. The night sky was now completely orange, as firelight radiated through the blowing smoke.

In between live shots, producer Bianca Seward and I jumped into our Wagoneer and drove down to Dead Man's Curve, through what felt like a tunnel of burning eucalyptus trees. *Just gun it.* At some point, Bianca asked me if I wanted her to drive, and I thanked her for the offer but explained that I could probably drive these roads with my eyes closed.

I stepped on the gas, fearing that embers would find their way into the SUV's engine. Bianca had never covered a fire before, and I had never driven through one like this. *Fuck it, we have to see what's going on.* We passed homes in flames on both sides of the street, passed Brooktree Road, the turn my parents would make when driving me to piano lessons when I was in elementary school, and made the climb to the intersection of Chautauqua and Sunset Boulevards, where our fears were confirmed. In front of us, the heart of Pacific Palisades—the village—was engulfed.

"We can't stay here," I told Bianca. Instead of attempting to set up shop, we made a U-turn and retreated back to the intersection of Amalfi and Sunset, orienting our vehicle in the direction away from the Palisades in case we needed to get out at a moment's notice.

"On the other side of that ridge right now," I explained to our audience, knowing full well that Lawrence didn't need any primer, "is the Palisades village. That was about as far as I've gone earlier this evening, but we had to turn around because there are homes in the Palisades village that—in the heart of this community—where there are shops, and a movie theater, and many schools. Palisades High School is there, Marquez Elementary School." I stopped short of a complete sentence as I was free associating what I knew to be in the path of the fire.

"Much of Pacific Palisades tonight is up in flames."

Like helicopter pilot Larry Welk, who was watching the Eaton Fire grow, I was hearing explosions of my own as Lawrence talked about how "thickly settled" the Palisades is—urban and dense. I thought the explosions were propane gas tanks. At least, that is what I told him. *Maybe they're electric car batteries?* I wondered. Whatever they were, they were astonishingly loud. As we continued to talk about the people who had left their cars and literally run for their lives away from the flames earlier in the day, another explosion happened somewhere behind me, at seven thirty on the dot. The LAPD cops shouted at people to get out and get away.

Earlier, I had told Lawrence about the firefighting efforts from the sky. "We've been watching those water air-drop airplanes and helicopters fly over this neighborhood." But none were visible at the moment. And I wondered why.

Just as the Eaton Fire had ignited uncomfortably close to the start of the earlier Kinneloa Fire, this wasn't the first "Palisades Fire" that had encroached upon and terrorized thousands of homes in the Highlands. In the fall of 2019 a blaze broke out at roughly the same time—around 10:40 a.m.—as the fire now engulfing an entire Los Angeles neighborhood, and it grew quickly to thirty acres on Palisades Drive, sending residents scrambling.

"A lot of parents are coming, but it's tough to get in and out," a father named Greg Philyan told the *Los Angeles Times* as he hiked up the street with his three-year-old on his shoulders after picking her up at Calvary Christian School, near the intersection of Sunset and Palisades Drive. "My first concern is it's going to come down the hill."

As he walked, "[A] helicopter doused flames across the road," the paper reported.

In that fire, two hundred homes were ordered to evacuate "the area bordered by Charmel Lane, Bienveneda Avenue, Merivale Lane, and Lachman Lane." None had burned. But tonight, if they hadn't already, it seemed like they would. A key difference? A little-known but crucial heliport—just like the one where Larry Welk was now waiting and watching for choppers above JPL—known as 69 Bravo.

With views that would rival those of any mansion in Los Angeles, the arial refueling base at Saddle Peak in the Santa Monica Mountains—between the Palisades and Malibu—is part of a massive property owned by a former radio executive. Working with the Los Angeles County Fire Department, he transformed a portion of it into one of the most critical firefighting assets in Los Angeles, where helicopters could "snorkel" thousands of gallons of water from orange aboveground water tanks known as "pumpkins" dozens of times a day to fight fires from the sky that were otherwise unreachable.

In the case of the 2019 Palisades Fire, the base proved invaluable, "as drought and sanitation efforts, such as the covering of Santa Ynez Reservoir in Palisades Highlands," the *Los Angeles Times* wrote then of the 117-million-gallon reservoir, "have made other water sources less accessible."

On January 7, 2025, the same reservoir was offline for repairs, making 69 Bravo's role again central to the initial air attack on the Palisades Fire and raising questions about the consequences of such a large water source so close to the fire being unavailable when it was seemingly needed most. LAFD chief pilot Dan Child, who was in the sky in the HLCO command-and-control role, was listening for reports from the outpost. But as conditions continued to deteriorate, he started thinking about doing something he had never done in his career.

How do I just cancel aircraft for the night? Are we here just to put water in the air, or are we here trying to get water to the ground? At what point is it unsafe for the aircraft to be up here? We know this is super challenging. We're going to keep going until we're called off. And that guy to call it off is going to be myself.

At around seven thirty, Child looked at his HLCO officer and made the call.

"I'm gonna cancel all the aircraft."

"Yep, sounds good to me," he replied.

Child keyed in his radio.

"All aircraft assigned to the Palisades Fire, from HLCO, all air assets are being grounded for the night, return back to base."

Call after call came back in.

"Roger."

"Copy."

"We'll see you tomorrow."

It was the last thing these firefighters wanted to hear. They love flying: the adrenaline rush and the fear and stress that come with what they call the "pucker factor." But tonight they knew how little they were able to impact the fire and how dangerous it was to be in the sky above it. It was time to pack it up. No night vision goggles or amount of horsepower could mitigate the winds they were facing.

At the Eaton Fire, just an hour after ignition, aircraft there—facing similar conditions—were grounded as well.

Cate Heneghan was familiar with a different type of flight. In her day job at NASA's Jet Propulsion Laboratory, she coordinates and organizes specialized engineers on spaceflight missions. She had also, outside of her work at JPL, trained as an EMT and joined Los Angeles County's Community Emergency Response Team, or CERT, learning the basics of disaster response and emergency management. Suspecting that the Eaton Fire would spread rapidly, her training and instincts kicked in. Around eight in the evening, she started checking on her McNally Avenue neighbors on the north end of the block. Another McNally resident kept tabs on the folks at the south end.

The block was close-knit and diverse. There were retirees, young children, immigrants, people who spoke little English. There were neighbors who'd lived there less than a year, and neighbors who'd been there their whole lives—one woman still lived in the house her parents bought in the 1960s. Some, like Loyda and Herb Wilson, were out of town. Others, like Mike and Monique Bagby, were at home and seemed like they weren't going to go anywhere. At least one woman was heading to bed, unaware of the fire until Cate Heneghan knocked on her door.

At this point, if any of their cars were inside an automatic garage, it would need to be opened manually in order to pack and get ready to leave. Heneghan didn't believe a fire could reach McNally, but the smoke and winds were unrelenting, so she started gathering more essentials. A cot. A camping mat. A sleeping bag. The sentimental items—things that were invaluable or irreplaceable—weren't even on her radar. She could have put them in a small box.

I'll only need to be out of here for a few days or weeks—if the smoke damage gets bad.

11

“Abandon the Station”

AS EIGHT THIRTY APPROACHED, IT OCCURRED TO ME and our team that a heavy smoke had settled in over the intersection of Amalfi Drive and Sunset Boulevard, where we had been sitting tight for hours. The incandescent light of the fires was barely visible through the thick, black haze, and streetlights, the headlights of emergency response vehicles, and even porch lights cast beams as if they were lighthouses shining into the darkness of the ocean. We couldn’t see the fire, but the wind was blowing stronger than at any point since we’d arrived on the scene.

As I waited to join the MSNBC broadcast, Stephanie Ruhle teased an upcoming report about the fires raging in the city. But her show started with a story about Mark Zuckerberg announcing an end to fact-checking on Facebook in favor of a “community notes” system similar to the one Elon Musk was employing on his social media site, X, formerly Twitter. I didn’t have the time or the bandwidth to think about the report and certainly didn’t believe it had anything to do with the calamity taking place before my eyes.

When she got to me, Steph, with whom I had once participated in a Mother’s Day event at 30 Rock with both of our moms, started by asking me about my family.

“How are your parents, your siblings? What’s going on with you?”

Before I could answer, both of the lapels on my yellow Nomex jacket started to quiver like chattering lips in freezing cold. The Velcro strap on my left shoulder meant to close the collar around my neck if fire overtook me flapped upward toward my face.

"Everybody's OK, thank God," I said, as a gust stronger than any I had experienced barreled through. I squinted, leaned into the wind, and angled my body to be as parallel with the ground as I could while standing upright and holding the stick mic.

"You can see—you used the word *windstorm*," I said, referring back to her introduction as debris blew by. "It's like a firestorm."

A gust knocked me back on my heels as I started to explain why the sky behind me didn't look bright orange like it had earlier in the evening.

"You can't see it behind me right now, but there is a lot of fire in all of that black smoke."

No sooner did those words leave my mouth than the sky became a brighter gradient of black-to-red-to-orange than it had been all night. That Velcro patch flipped up again, this time sticking to my cheek, pressed there firmly by the wind.

"I think we throw around *unprecedented* often, Steph. I have never in my life seen a storm like this in Los Angeles.

"On the other side of town, where I live today—I was talking to my wife earlier this evening—there's a fire burning in Altadena. Opposite side of Los Angeles County from where we are right now. Trees are falling down. Particulate matter is blowing through the air. This is a very dangerous situation," I relayed as embers blew between me and the camera, and directly behind me. I was thinking specifically of what my wife told me had happened at our house: In a video she took just after seven and texted me, you could see the aftermath of a five- or six-foot-long branch from a massive pine tree in our neighbor's yard that had blown off, flown over the fence in between our homes, and shattered not only the table in our yard but twisted beyond repair the steel chairs that surrounded it. Based on the damage, I worried it could have killed someone—her or one of our kids—if they had been standing under it when it fell.

As I turned to look back over my left shoulder, describing "almost a twister of sorts" that we had been experiencing, flames became visible closer to us than we had seen them yet. I rubbed my nose, revealing to the audience that on my arm was a mask I had started to use off camera because of the smoke's effect on our lungs. Steph asked if I was worried about people who had not yet evacuated.

"If you are sitting at home watching MSNBC right now and you live in Pacific Palisades or the western part of Los Angeles and are under the mandatory evacuation order, turn off your television, get in your car, and get out of the area that you are in. This is incredibly, incredibly dangerous.

"This is a massive fire over a massive footprint, and it's only going to get larger over the course of this evening."

Steph asked me about whether or not I would be able to get home tonight after MSNBC switched from live coverage to repeats of the primetime broadcasts, which end at midnight on the East Coast. I couldn't fathom that there was anywhere to go—that the fire was continuing to grow out of control—so I told her we'd stay put for now.

"I love you. Please stay safe," Steph said to me.

"Thank you, my friend."

At the same moment we got off the air, the Pasadena Park Healthcare and Wellness Center was evacuating residents in wheelchairs, on stretchers, and with walkers—some hooked up to oxygen tanks—as embers blew around them, less than a mile from where

Chief Garcia and the incident command center had fled due to the danger of the approaching fire.

Vans, ambulances, a bus, and even a tactical SWAT vehicle were being used to transport anyone and everyone from the facility—as well as from a neighboring nursing home, The Terraces at Park Marino—away from the area as conditions deteriorated by the second.

The smoke was so thick that Macy Jenkins, a reporter for KNBC on the scene, couldn't even see the flames that were the cause of it. An engine from Los Angeles County Fire Station No. 165—dispatched from around twenty miles away in Huntington Park—pulled up. Immediately, a firefighter yanked the hose off the vehicle, threw it over his left shoulder, and hiked up the sidewalk and out of sight as he and the others in his company did what they could to protect the facility from a fire that had grown to at least four hundred acres.

In the Palisades, Eric Mendoza and other members of Sixty-Nines had been fighting the fire on their stomachs in the middle of the street for hours. Mendoza had been able to run into a house to wash his eyes out and take whatever gulp of water he could with the water supply shut off to homes.

The Palisades Presbyterian Church, near where he had left the ladder truck with tiller wheels in the center divider, was at risk of catching fire. A maintenance worker from the high school was there with a garden hose trying to protect it as the office building next to it burned.

Mendoza was beat. Done. Nevertheless, he and the rest of his company deployed the heaviest hose they had—two and a half inches in diameter—on both structures.

We are not going to let this church burn down.

Back in the village, where Station No. 69 was situated, just about anything that could burn there had started burning. But Mendoza and everyone else stayed. *Crazy* is how Mendoza thought the fire was behaving, but they kept fighting hard for a knockout blow on the church's office complex. Eventually Mendoza contained the office fire and got the win he was looking for.

Captain Jeff Brown told Mendoza that he was going to head back closer to the station to check on reports of homes burning nearby.

Mendoza followed, heading to his ladder truck, which was still running and had been for the hours since they left it in the middle of Sunset.

Thank God it's still there.

Captain Brown, once near the station house, radioed back to the men he had left behind to relay that homes were indeed burning, and they were pivoting to structure protection there.

Mendoza and Mike Romero, the apparatus operator on his truck, hit the road in that direction. Exhaustion and adrenaline were fiercely battling each other as they rolled through smoke-shrouded streets. They managed to join other engines fighting fires at apartment complexes along Sunset near Temescal Canyon, but realized that they couldn't get through—their truck was too big.

They needed to get to Sixty-Nines. But the way there was obstructed not only by other companies but also by power lines. They tried to get back by creeping through small side streets.

Homes engulfed. Roads blocked.

"We can't get through. We've got to back down."

"Eric! There's power lines," Romero shouted.

Mendoza, who had been an electrical lineman early in his professional career, knew what to look out for. He knew what would electrocute him and what wouldn't. What a comms line was and what would shock the life out of him. So, he climbed out of his bucket and started grabbing downed wires lying in the street. Lifting them. Driving over them. Eventually they reached Pacific Coast Highway, where they could take the long way around and back up into the village to get to their fire station, all the while surrounded by flames.

Once they climbed Chautauqua Boulevard, the windy road that ascends several hundred feet from the coast to Sunset, they swung the truck left.

Everything's on fire.

Homes on both sides of the street were ablaze. To Mendoza, it felt as though a blowtorch were shooting across the street.

"What are we going to do?" Romero asked.

"I'm burning in this bucket," he said from the tiller bucket atop the back of the fire truck.

It's so hot.

Looking down, it was as if the paint itself inside the truck was melting. Mendoza, who had his brush helmet on, ducked down on the steering wheel.

"Floor it! I'm burning!"

Romero maneuvered the truck onto the opposite side of the street—his best bet to see anything through the heavy smoke and flames—pushing the engine as fast as it would go.

"Mike, just go! Go!"

Romero punched through the torch, while Mendoza tillered on his side to avoid flames coming through the window.

I'm melted. My helmet is shot on one side.

Navigating through intense flames, they made it back to Station No. 69 and parked the truck facing toward the village, lights still flashing. With embers blowing in all directions, they ran inside the station, which was now at risk of going up. Mendoza started shooting water from inside of the station outside to create a water curtain to stop embers from blowing inside. But confidence was low, and an order came across to prepare to evacuate.

"Grab your personal stuff!" someone shouted. "Grab your wallets! Everything from the station. We're going to abandon the station. The station is going to burn."

No it's not, Mendoza thought. Instead, he and others fighting the fire moved their cars across the street to the open parking lot at Ralphs supermarket, where bushes were on fire, but the structure and the massive lot seemed safe. On the street, one of the only details the human eye could see other than flames were the historic Marbelite 800 streetlights that line the roads of the Palisades, many of them installed just years after the community's founding, around 1928. Magically, a number of them still had power that night. Author India Mandelkern describes the concrete-poled, glass-topped objects of simple but elegant beauty in her history of Los Angeles streetlights, *Electric Moons*:

> Marbelite 800 rewards the streetlight chaser who cares to give it a second look. . . . [I]t sports a geometric collar around its neck, but don't miss the delicate meandering band just underneath the luminaire. Let your eyes wander to its circular base, decorated with bas-relief carvings of laurel wreaths.

Running my fingers down the side of one of these lights still elicits a sensory memory. After nearly a century, they had some jagged edges, but they felt so good, and so familiar, and so much like the Palisades. Now they were beacons of survival—at least the ones that hadn't lost power yet—held high by a material that would withstand even the most ferocious of blazes.

As gusts across the ridgetops above the Palisades reached ninety-eight miles per hour after ten o'clock, and the Marbelites stood tall as the homes around them smoldered, Mendoza moved his hose back and forth out the back of the station between the houses while trying to keep the water curtain intact.

12

"I'm Losing the Whole Block"

BY TEN IN THE EVENING, THE EATON FIRE COMMAND post had been repositioned yet again—this time to the Rose Bowl parking lot in Pasadena. With the neon marquee of the legendary football stadium hovering over them in the near distance, emergency officials from across Los Angeles County huddled to strategize how to attack the fire without air assets and with wind speeds increasing.

Robert Garcia of the Forest Service was there, and amassed with him were the fire chiefs for the cities of Arcadia and Sierra Madre, the incident commander for the county of Los Angles and for the Forest Service, the deputy fire chief for the city of Pasadena, and representatives of the state's Office of Emergency Management, the Los Angeles County Sheriff's Office, and the Pasadena Police Department. Finally, all of the key players, in one place that was out of harm's way, working on a unified command, with hundreds of acres of open space at their disposal.

Less than four miles away, many of Cate Heneghan's neighbors had left McNally Avenue by the time the command post was established at the Rose Bowl. Despite confidence that the fire wouldn't reach their block, with no power and smoke filling the air, friends' homes with electricity were more attractive than waiting out the night on the block. But Heneghan decided to do just that.

As long as the air is clear and I can see the fire, I'm OK.

Four miles south of McNally Avenue, and across the street from the Pasadena Jewish Temple and Center, now ablaze, Bruce Costantino, a middle-aged man wearing a red flannel jacket, a gaiter around his neck, and ski goggles atop his bushy, grey hair, was using a garden hose to put out embers on an apartment complex he owned along Altadena Drive.

"I really hope I'm helping. I'm really quick to leave if it gets any more sketchy than it is," he told Macy Jenkins of KNBC. "But I feel like I'm helping."

Jenkins, as she tossed back to the anchors now in the studio across from my office at Universal, felt a worrying shove. "The wind is pushing us south. I can feel it."

Gavin Newsom was holed up at the exclusive Beverly Hilton Hotel in Beverly Hills, his team having commandeered three conference rooms as a command center for the governor's office. From here, they could videoconference with his emergency operations team, which was primarily up in Sacramento, and prepare to request a major disaster declaration from the Biden White House. That night, Newsom's office announced that the state had secured a Federal Emergency Management Agency reimbursement guarantee called a Fire Management Assistance Grant for the Eaton Fire, after having received the same for the Palisades Fire earlier Tuesday.

With Joe Biden remaining overnight in Los Angeles—he was scheduled to meet his first great-grandchild the following morning—Newsom was able to brief him by phone. Biden had repeatedly reached out to Newsom as he received reports of the fire.

"Hey, we'd love to—I'd love to come down," the president said. "Let me check. That would be amazing."

Newsom, after consulting with his team, told Biden that going into the fire zone would be a drain on resources, but that they could meet in a nearby location, in Santa Monica, outside the zone.

"I totally understand," Biden conceded. "My folks are telling me the same thing."

"I think it'd be amazing if you could meet with some of these first responders right on the scene and brief you," Newsom told Biden.

Newsom knew that with the destruction continuing to escalate all evening and into the morning, a federal disaster declaration would be critical to jump-starting a recovery that was still off in the distance. Newsom, consulting with the White House, said he would like to present the declaration to Biden in person, so that the president would approve it in short order.

Disaster declarations are normally lengthy documents, but Newsom was advised by Biden's team that absent a full document, anything in writing would suffice. So Newsom decided to deliver it by hand to President Biden in the morning.

Just after 11 p.m., Joe Everett, assistant fire chief of the Los Angeles Fire Department and the incident commander for the Palisades Fire, found himself in the heart of the community for the first time. At the intersection of Chautauqua Boulevard and Sunset, he ran into KNBC reporter Robert Kovacik, with whom he spoke as homes burned on all sides of him, and the streets filled with water that was being sprayed in a futile effort to stop the ferocious blaze.

"As far as brush fires are concerned, this is one that I never wanted to see," the veteran firefighter admitted, looking ashen and dejected as he wore his white helmet, signifying his leadership role, with his yellow fireproof jacket unzipped over his black uniform.

"I pray for the fellow Angelenos. This is the area that I serve. I happen to be the incident commander right now. Unfortunately for me and my fellow neighbors here, it's one of the worst brush fires I've been in command with or actually been involved with. So, it's just . . . a number of things came together, and it's just a terrible storm that came through here, and we're just trying to pick up the pieces the best we can."

He continued: "We predicted some very high winds, and, like I said earlier, all it takes is a start, and that's what happened. This fire is spotting five miles ahead of us. Three miles ahead of us. It's extremely hard to put our arms around it. But like I said, we're doing the best we can."

"You're doing more than the best, Joe," Kovacik said.

"I appreciate that," the assistant chief replied, shaking the reporter's hand, then walking back to the ongoing firefight that Mendoza and the members of Sixty-Nines were still battling less than a half mile away.

As the Palisades continued to burn, there was an announcement of yet another fire breaking out: a hundred-acre blaze in Sylmar, the northernmost neighborhood in the city of Los Angeles—and word the Eaton Fire in Altadena had now grown to more than a thousand acres.

"Lord, let us save just one more house. Just give us a break," firefighter Tim Larson prayed in the cul-de-sac they had been defending for some twelve hours in the Palisades Highlands. As the winds began to shift 180 degrees in the late evening, and fire moved from the backyards to the front yards of homes, the engineer Larson, responsible for pumping water for the attack, and the rest of Twenty-Threes still had water pressure, but he was running out of another valuable resource: fuel. He'd arrived on the scene with a full tank: sixty gallons. Now it was virtually empty.

In thirty-five years with the LAFD, Larson had never been on an initial attack that lasted as long. He had to man a hose line himself because of the fire, but his "little engine" was running out of gas.

Man, if we run out of fuel, we're not gonna be able to get back up, Larson thought, knowing that a mechanic would then be needed to prime the fuel pump in the truck. *And now those houses are really gonna burn.*

He broke off the hose lines and raced the fire truck down Palisades Drive to a makeshift fuel station on the Pacific Coast Highway across from the legendary and recently-shuttered biker outpost Patrick's Roadhouse. On the drive, he saw for the first time the abandoned cars and the crush of humanity that had transpired a half day earlier.

At the station, he was met with a long line of fire apparatus waiting for gas.

"Hey, man, I'm gonna run out of fuel—on fumes."

They let him cut the line.

"Hurry up, hurry up. Put fuel in there. Put fuel in there."

They did, and by the time he made it back up to the Highlands and again hooked up his hose line to the hydrant, he discovered another dwindling resource.

Ain't no pressure.

When he opened the hydrant, he was able to get just enough water into the truck's intake to fill it up. But that was it. About 500 gallons, and for a hose line putting out around 125 or 200 gallons a minute, it was nothing.

Luckily, water tenders soon arrived on the scene.

"Hey, just stay here," Larson told the driver, whom he knew. "Just sit here."

As he heard reports from closer to the center of the Palisades, Larson and the other five men he was fighting the fire with hunkered down.

"Tim, we just got to hang on to these houses for another freaking day," a fellow firefighter told him. "Just another."

Meanwhile, distressing calls were coming in over the radio.

"I need as many resources you can get. I'm losing the whole block."

This is bad, Larson thought.

And in the village, it was bad.

Mendoza and Sixty-Nines all ran back across the street when it was clear that the Ralphs parking lot was no longer a safe place to keep their vehicles—the supermarket was now on fire. As were many of the homes they had tried to protect. Only two, directly adjacent to the station itself, were not ablaze.

13

"Oh My God"

UNLIKE CATE HENEGHAN, MCNALLY AVENUE RESIDENTS Herb and Loyda Wilson were over 2,500 miles away in Hawaii when the Eaton Fire exploded. They were helpless in a place that had recently faced one of the deadliest fires in modern US history. The 2023 fire in Lahaina, a small city on the island of Maui, was so devastating that human remains and burned-out homes were virtually indistinguishable to the untrained eye. People leaped into the Pacific Ocean to avoid burning to death in the flames. Now neighbors on their own block back home were considering when they would have to run.

The Wilsons visited Maui around ten times over the years as owners of a time share situated in the community of Kapalua. They were crushed by what they saw when they returned to the island in late 2023, just months after the fire. A routine visit to Lahaina's Front Street was made impossible in the aftermath of the search and recovery effort and subsequent debris removal process run by the US Army Corps of Engineers.

Herb, a retired longtime UPS employee, and Loyda, an El Salvador native who fled violence in her home country and later become a US citizen, first learned in a text message from Loyda's sister what was happening in Altadena, where they lived just down the block from Cate Heneghan. Their daughter Ashley, who had been dog-sitting their ten-year-old, hundred-pound Akita named Rosie, evacuated the house not long after the fire started.

"We'll deal with it when we get home," her dad told her, sending Ashley and Rosie back to her apartment in Pasadena.

Herb downloaded the Genasys Protect app and tracked the fire from his phone into the overnight hours as they watched the news.

"If we can get through the night, we should be OK," he told Loyda.

But by 11 p.m. in Altadena, the fire had crossed Lake Avenue, just a mile from their home. By then, only five of the twenty-four houses on their street were still occupied.

Cate Heneghan was still there, waiting for a sign she needed to leave. Not until two thirty in the morning did she get it, in the form of a scent. She knew that the particular smell of the smoke was not simply a brush fire.

It's toxic.

At the same time, I was on my way back to the Palisades after briefly returning home following my last live MSNBC report on Tuesday night. Our broadcast didn't go into the overnight hours as Bianca, J.B., Alan, and I had suspected it might, so we planned to meet back there early in the morning to see if we could push farther into the Palisades, or what was left of it.

When I made it home, I washed and dried my clothes, reeking of smoke, and slept, if you could call it sleep, on my couch not wanting to wake up my wife or the kids before rising again around one in the morning to shower and put back on those same clothes. Then off in the Wagoneer to pick up Bianca near Mid-City and make our way back to the Palisades to report live for the *Today* show.

It was Wednesday, January 8. I texted Bianca, letting her know that I was awake and getting ready to head back to pick her up. Both her home and mine were in parts of Los Angeles where fire had not reached, but it felt like we were in a horror movie. Streets deserted. Debris everywhere. The smell of smoke wafted through the city.

"ETA 2:20."

By 2:52 a.m., we were again rounding Dead Man's Curve, passing Will Rogers State Historic Park on our right, talking with J.B. and Alan over the radio as they trailed behind us. The street was littered with debris—primarily downed tree limbs. I wasn't sure if we'd be able to make it all the way into the village based on what we had seen the night before.

"We've got flames even right there, too," Bianca said, pointing out a fire burning below a massive sycamore tree, stripped of all of its leaves.

To our left was a home that had burned down almost entirely; only the frame was left standing, and it, too, was engulfed.

"Dude, I mean . . ." Bianca trailed off.

"Onward, forward. Onward, forward," I radioed to the guys behind us.

Sunset Boulevard was on fire on both sides of this windy stretch below the park and before we'd climb into the village.

"That's awful, man."

"Holy shit," Bianca let out.

"Look at this tree."

"I know."

"Fuck, dude." I didn't really have any other words. "Tree fell down," I said, swerving around it.

We passed the entrance to Will Rogers on Sunset and carried on farther. As we rounded a bend, the scene before us was suddenly illuminated bright orange.

"Oh, boy."

To our right a group of houses was actively burning—the light source we had just noticed.

"Holy crap," Bianca said.

"Keep going, keep going, keep going," I said into the radio and stepped on it as we started the climb into the village and dodged another downed tree. Above us was what was left of the iconic Robert Bridges House, the wood-and-glass structure that had hung over Sunset for decades on massive concrete stilts. *The New York Times* had profiled it in 2014:

> The home does have an air of mystery. Its dramatic form and remote perch suggest the lair of a Bond villain or an aging Hollywood producer-turned-recluse. It is a striking example of brutalism, yet it isn't the work of a renowned architect and doesn't appear on greatest-hit lists of the city's modernist masterworks.

It had always seemed indestructible to me. Now the landmark was gone.

We passed Chautauqua Boulevard and were now driving deeper into the Palisades than we had the night before. What are you supposed to say when the entire community you were born and raised in is wiped off the map, literally burning to the ground before your eyes? I couldn't come up with much.

"Oh my God. Oh. My. God."

On our right, as far as we could see into what is known as the Alphabet Streets of the Palisades, not one home was left standing. Only debris and flames and the silhouettes of once lush trees now reduced to twigs. Directly in front of us, not a single light was on—no power anywhere—but the entire horizon was lit and glowing orange. What looked like dozens of fire trucks were visible in the distance, right where I knew Fire Station No. 69 to be.

"This is so sad," I let out.

All of the Marbelite streetlamps were dark. Chimneys stood at attention. The homes they were once attached to were gone. Multiple houses on the left-hand side of the street were still engulfed. But we pressed forward. Rivers of water lapped at the curb on both sides, reflecting the colors of the flames. As we passed the shell of a home to our left that was still spewing flames out of the window frames, I wondered out loud about what we were seeing ahead.

"Did the fire station burn down? Oh my God! This is the fire station," I told Bianca about No. 69. It was still intact. "They protected it so far—it looks like."

Embers were floating onto our car from a tree next door to the station. Outside, firefighters from Nines and Tens, both from downtown Los Angeles, and Elevens, from MacArthur Park, were protecting the station. We swerved around them to the left, into the oncoming traffic lanes. Sitting outside the station were four firefighters, some still wearing their helmets. The garage door was shut.

On our left, we passed directly by Eric Mendoza's truck, now pressed up against the curb—the aftermath of the unsuccessful firefight to save the Ralphs supermarket.

"Oh. My. God," I said again as we traveled farther into the village. Our old First Federal Bank, on the right, gone.

"This is awful, dude."

On the right, I noticed billionare developer Rick Caruso's shopping center, Palisades Village, still standing. On the left, just across Sunset, the historic Palisades Business Block, as it was officially known, was only a burning facade.

"That's got to be a hundred years old."

"What is it?" Bianca asked.

"It's so sad," I said, either not hearing her or not being able to answer. Through the archways that framed what was most recently a Starbucks, fire was visible shooting through and up out of the roof. The Italian restaurant next door and the Bank of America, gone too. An American flag was flying—though almost stick-straight—as the winds blew west toward the ocean, moving with it embers from inside the building.

"This is Caruso's property," I explained to Bianca about what was on our right. "Is it on fire at all?" It didn't seem to be. I did not notice the private firefighting force he had hired to defend it.

I made a U-turn in the middle of Swarthmore and Sunset—the intersection I had wanted to make it to but failed to around twelve hours earlier.

"This is a very historic building," I remarked about what we were witnessing, now on our right-hand side. I stopped the car, rolled down my window, and took a photo at 3:36 a.m. We returned to Chautauqua and Sunset where, with NBC technical engineer Dan Peterson, we picked a location where we could go live on the *Today* show within the next hour. I posted the photo to my Instagram account with a simple caption:

> The Village. 3:36 a.m. 💔

On the corner of Pampas Ricas and Sunset, houses were on fire on every corner. Using a Starlink portable satellite, Dan established a broadcast signal for us. Then we waited in the car to spare ourselves from the choking smoke as much as possible until it was time to go on air. I had just under an hour until I would be live in front of millions of people on the *Today* show. Just under an hour to sit with my thoughts, trapped in the eye-watering haze that had seeped into the car, as ashes of my hometown fluttered down on the windshield in front of me.

* * *

As morning encroached upon night in Altadena, Cate Heneghan prepared herself.

Houses are burning nearby.

She drew a map of McNally, so that she could visualize who was still there after checking in on her neighbors. She couldn't see fire outside her home—smoke had concealed what was happening beyond McNally. She was ready to go.

As she approached her Subaru, she suddenly remembered that while repairing her car a few days earlier, she'd removed the driver's side door panel as well as the exterior door handle. She was going to put everything back together the following weekend. Instead, she put the handle back on and threw the interior panel in the back seat, leaving around three in the morning on Wednesday. As she pulled away, she stopped to urge one of her neighbors to leave. She then headed to an emergency shelter, not knowing when she would be able to return home.

A half hour later, in Hawaii, her neighbors Loyda and Herb received another cell phone alert: The fire had spread to Mendocino Street and Visscher Place, just a few blocks away from McNally.

"I don't think we're going to make it," Loyda said glumly as they sat in the Hawaiian darkness, while the Eaton Fire was racing toward the Altadena home they had lived in for twenty-one years.

Around that time, the firefighters of the Los Angeles County Fire Department's Twelves were ordered away from the initial attack area in Eaton Canyon and toward the residents of McNally Avenue.

14

"We Are Safe"

AT 3:34 A.M. I TEXTED MY FAMILY THE SAME PHOTO I had posted to Instagram of the historic "pink building," as everyone called it, in the center of the Palisades. The Palisades Business Block was the original center of town a hundred years earlier and a hub of our family's life in the Palisades for many years—countless Italian dinners, ATM withdrawals, and coffee runs. We used to use the parking lot on the side, in between the pink building and our old pediatrician's office, to go to our favorite restaurants in town: Café Vida and Cathay Palisades, a local Chinese restaurant which had shut down in 2022.

> Entire palisades village is gone. This was Starbucks just drove through
>
> Houses all along sunset gone
>
> Huntington houses burned every street

"Oh my Gd," my brother Miles, who was awake with his wife after having left behind everything they owned, wrote back.

"Omg," Shana texted.

"It's horrible," I replied. "I'm at Chautauqua and Sunset. Every house in the intersection on fire." I continued:

Will stay here for now

We are safe in good shape with fire teams etc

All the firefighters are gathered around to save the fire station

"Wow," said Miles.

"Yes, please stay safe," Shana urged.

I got out of the car on Chautauqua and went around the corner to Pampas Ricas, just a few houses off Sunset Boulevard. I was an eight-minute walk from the house I was born into but hadn't yet been able to see, looking to pick a live shot location for the *Today* show. Anywhere would have sufficed because everything *everywhere* was on fire. The crackling was so loud and the noises created by the flames destroying homes were so intense I pressed my earpiece in harder than usual to make sure I heard cohosts Savannah Guthrie, Hoda Kotb, and Craig Melvin back in studio 1A as they introduced me from New York.

"Jacob, what are you seeing?" Guthrie asked.

"Savannah, Hoda, Craig, this is an absolutely catastrophic, devastating situation." I had goggles over my glasses to protect my eyes from smoke and an NBC News baseball cap on my head to protect my hair from catching fire. Wrapped around my right hand, which was holding the stick microphone, was an N95 mask I had been wearing until the moment I went on air.

"This is a neighborhood—a wonderful neighborhood." An explosion popped off somewhere around me, but amid all the other audible destruction, it was hard to register exactly what it was. So I carried on. "It happens to be the neighborhood I was born and raised in.

"You look around, and everywhere you look all you see is homes on fire. There's two behind me here," I said, moving to the other side of the street as Alan Rice followed with his camera.

There, only the facade of a home—the garage, windows, and a basketball hoop out front—remained standing as flames jumped outward through every possible opening.

"It is not an exaggeration to say that it has not just been a windstorm, it has been a consistent and very dangerous firestorm," I said, repeating what had become clear hours earlier. "Much of Pacific Palisades is burning as I speak to you this morning, you guys."

In another time, at another moment, the street I was reporting from would be sealed off not because the neighborhood was combusting in front of me but because it was along the route of the annual Fourth of July road race through the Palisades. I stood there, clearing our television airwaves in air that was anything but clean, putting my mask back on and thinking about all of the places within minutes of me that were no longer.

With time to kill before my next on-air appearance, Bianca and I got back into the Wagoneer, which we had kept running with the windows closed to keep out the smoke—a futile effort—and drove again into the heart of the village. For the first time, I laid eyes on what was happening off of Sunset, behind the pink building and deeper into the neighborhood. The entire block of Antioch Street was on fire. Café Vida. The old Cathay Palisades. All of the retail businesses across the street. Only the palm trees and utility poles were standing. Barely. On lower Swarthmore, Beech Street Café, where I would get my favorite pizza—the Bianca, with garlic cream sauce, ricotta, spinach, and mozzarella, a staple of many sleepovers and friend hangs—was still aflame, reduced to a pile. Village School was on fire, too.

As we returned toward our live shot position, we swung by the local public library. The flags on the pole were waving, standing, like the one over the pink building, parallel to the ground thrust by the wind. Below them, the books inside were now fuel—a real-life *Fahrenheit 451* playing out under the dark sky thick with smoke.

When we pulled back up to our location, and as I waited to go live again for our streaming network, a large yellow truck from the California Office of Emergency Services drove past. On air moments later, words came out of my mouth, but I was not fully able to grasp the severity of the situation. As soon as I was off the air, I took out my cell phone and recorded a selfie video. It was 5:51 a.m. I was thinking of my family. My childhood best friend Sean. Kids I might have played with at the park. All of it.

"Hey. This is a message for my Palisades people," I said, my mouth covered by my N95, eyes shielded by both my glasses and goggles, and my hat turned around backward. The collar of my yellow Nomex jacket was lifted up by the breeze as embers swirled, the wind blew, and the massive trees behind me practically begged not to be ignited by the house fires burning below them.

"It's a really tough situation out here. I'm on Pampas Ricas, where Sunset meets Chautauqua. I drove into the village earlier. Um, most of the houses on Sunset between"—I inhaled sharply, trying to catch my breath not because of the smoke or heat but because I was processing what I was about to say out loud—"Chautauqua and the village have burned down. On both sides of the street. The firefighters are trying to save the fire station. Ralphs is burned down. Gelson's is burned down," I said of our local supermarkets as ash and embers blew in multiple directions directly around and over and across my body.

"The car wash. The library. The whole area where the park is. In the Huntington," the name for the part of the Palisades where I was standing, "many of the streets are on fire. Alphabet Streets," I said of the area behind the fire station scared to say what I had really seen—there was nothing left. "I just hope everybody got out OK and everyone is looking after one another. Just wanted to send my love."

I tapped my heart with my left hand twice and looked off into the distance, lowering the phone and stopping the recording. I was with colleagues, and other media, and firefighters. I wanted to be home. Home in my house on the other side of town, where my wife, Nicole, and our kids had evacuated from because of the smoke. Home in my first childhood house, which I was almost sure had burned down. Home with my mom and my dad and my brother and three sisters. Adrenaline wearing thin, I felt truly alone, isolated, and scared. And fire was everywhere.

On Homewood Drive in Altadena at 5:23 a.m., the entire block of massive, hulking trees, wide streets, and mansion-sized homes set back from long driveways was helpless in the face of the powerful wind and flames. The street was lined by palm trees, thirteen of them practically stooped over; they resembled bows without arrows. The center of the road was dark, illuminated in the distance with the orange glow of whatever was burning ahead. A KNBC news crew was there, walking westbound toward more danger they could sense but not see.

Just over two miles in that direction was McNally Avenue. Loyda and Herb Wilson, on Maui, and Cate Heneghan found out their block was burning as neighbors relayed messages to one another. Mike and Monique Bagby, the last to leave their house on the block, waited until flames made it to McNally around 5:35 a.m. Herb knew that was it. Mike had stayed, a sign of hope from an ocean away, since they knew he was a bit of a chicken. He had even let Monique fall asleep for a while. But on the phone across the Pacific, there was no question things were dire.

"Ashes. I've gotta go," Mike told Herb. Soon, in a group text to their neighbors, Monique shared the scene on their street as they escaped under the giant oak trees that line the block.

> A small fire by the curb and embers were blowing off it. As we made a left on Fairoaks, we saw a fire truck and told him about it and he said we have no resources.

Cate was in her car somewhere in Burbank, where some friends had pulled up side by side to get some rest. Herb and Loyda started working on plans to make it back to Altadena as quickly as possible, searching for plane tickets online, though they didn't know what they would find, if anything, when they arrived.

Devastating was the first word that came to mind at 6:36 a.m., as I joined the *Morning Joe* program on MSNBC twenty-four minutes before the sun was supposed to come up. Mika Brzezinski was in the anchor chair. Embers flew horizontally past my face, seemingly bouncing off the ski-style goggles I had fastened tightly around my glasses. The smoke was starting to burn my eyes and lungs, but for the TV hit, I had pulled down my mask.

"Everywhere you look, there are homes on fire. We're talking about dozens, if not . . . hundreds?"

I knew that I was underestimating.

"There are tens of thousands of people that are displaced right now."

As I ran through my TV-friendly recap of my community and its destruction, it occurred to me that I was on the Beltway's favorite morning show—and that now would be an ideal time to talk about what it was going to take to start over.

"I know that there are a lot of policymakers who watch this

broadcast every single day, especially in Washington," I began. "The recovery from this is going to be one on the scale, I'd imagine, of the Big One—from the Earthquake," the natural disaster we have all been taught to fear and prepare for and expect in Los Angeles. "This is as bad as you can possibly imagine for a community anywhere in the country, much less in the heart of urban Los Angeles."

I could hear the anchors' deep sighs in my earpiece as they absorbed the gravity of the situation.

"Everywhere you look, things that made up this community, a very vibrant, very beautiful community in the heart of Los Angeles . . ." I paused and looked around to again absorb and respect and acknowledge the flames—a radiance so ugly and beautiful at the same time it was hard not to stare at.

Flames were ripping through another house behind me, the radiant heat making my back and neck uncomfortably hot. I inhaled a giant gulp of smoke, causing me to reflexively clear my throat. The particulate in the smoke was the likely culprit of my cough, though it, too, could have been my childhood memories trying to escape the tightness of my chest. I shook my head in disbelief—almost to push out the sentence I hadn't finished. It worked.

". . . is no longer this morning, Mika."

Political reporter and *Morning Joe* cohost Jonathan Lemire reminded me that the fires were still 0 percent contained. He asked what could be done to control the flames.

"Those aircraft will probably be back in the sky," I said, looking up into the smoky blackness, again clearing my throat of whatever was making its way inside, "as soon as day breaks here."

Part Two

Extended Attack

15

"It's Katie Miller"

JAKE LEVINE, THE SPECIAL ASSISTANT TO PRESIDENT Biden and my high school carpool passenger from the Palisades, had made it back to Washington, DC, and was preparing for a big day at the White House. He was about to walk into an important meeting—one of his final official duties of the administration—about Ukraine. But his mind was on the Palisades as he texted me to say that he thought his mom's house on El Medio was still standing, based on what he had seen on social media.

"Send me the address," I wrote back, thinking I would try to get there after the *Today* show. It was around six thirty in the morning.

Levine did, then put his phone into a cabinet outside of a SCIF, a sensitive compartmentalized information facility, inside the Eisenhower Executive Office Building on the White House grounds. The equivalent of the Situation Room in the White House, no electronic devices would be permitted due to the sensitive nature of the intelligence discussed inside.

As he and other high level officials discussed Ukraine, the sun rose over the Palisades, or over the smoke and haze blanketing the Palisades, at seven o'clock on the dot. Bianca and I had retreated to our Jeep again. When it was clear that the sky would provide us enough light to look around and that the dark, thick cloud of smoke wasn't going to be permanent, an adrenaline jolt or momentary flush of hope shot through my nervous system. I had to see what the Palisades looked like in daylight.

By 7:37 a.m., we were driving down Sunset into the village in our Wagoneer, which now smelled as if someone had smoked about five thousand cigarettes inside of it. I was at the wheel and had my head cocked to the south side of the street. In some places, remarkably, I could see the normal shade of grey the sky is at this hour just off the Pacific coast. Columns of darker grey smoke still rose above us. Not every house had burned—there were several still standing.

"Look at how that one house survived. Wow."

Winds were still whipping trees around.

"This one survived," I said a couple of doors down. "It's crazy."

For a moment, we sat in silence, absorbing the fact that there was virtually nothing left. On my left was a home still on fire, but on my right was Sixty-Nines—still standing.

"The fire station survived."

We passed an engine from Elevens that was sitting in the middle of the soaking-wet road, evidence of the overnight battle waged to save the station.

"Everything around it burned. Everything. Around. It. Burned."

My brother and his wife suspected that her parents' home, where they had been staying and had evacuated from, had burned down. But the fate of the house they had recently bought and were renovating ahead of the birth of their daughter was less clear—just down the canyon at the bottom of Bienveneda Avenue, on a side street. I told them I would take a look if we could get there, and Bianca agreed to accompany me.

As I drove, I texted my family chat about what survived—and what didn't.

Pali burned
The HS
KI is good

KI was our temple, Kehillat Israel, which had survived. The high school hadn't entirely, but buildings on its perimiter had. The Presbyterian church that Eric Mendoza and Sixty-Nines had tried to save had not. It took us around two minutes to get there from the fire station, and when we turned right onto Bienveneda, it was clear we wouldn't be able to drive the additional several blocks to my brother's house because power lines were down. I told Bianca that I was going to get out and run up the hill—and if she didn't hear from me in a few minutes to come find me. Smoke billowed from the direction of his home.

I started jogging up the street, the first time I had done anything other than walk slowly or sit in the car or stand around since our coverage began. I didn't need to run, but my body told me to do it. Trotting up the hill, I could see the thick smoke of an active fire, and to the left a crack of blue sky—the first I had seen. As I approached the small single-story home that was tucked behind a flesh-pink fence covered in vines and bougainvillea, my eyes first darted to what was happening across the street. Their neighbor's home was fully engulfed in fire—explosive flames leaped off the house—as if it had ignited in the time we had been driving there. Flames were absolutely ripping through the structure, and rising from the ground were blackened trees and the wood frame of whatever once stood there. That was it.

But across the street was my brother's house, seemingly untouched. The hedges. The wall. The curb. The wind wasn't done with their street yet, though. Knowing that Bianca was waiting for me, I snapped a couple of photos, turned around, and ran back to meet her.

"It's still there!" I told her. I texted my family chat with the pictures.

> Your house still standing guys but house across the street burning bad
>
> Pray for wind to push away

As I reported back on my family text chain, KNBC, which had been on the air for twenty hours straight without commercial interruption, returned to its news crew on the scene. Reporter Michelle Valles was about three miles to the east of where Twelves was fighting to save homes and their station itself. Firefighter Gunner Alves was on the pitched roof of the station in an hours-long battle, while a fellow firefighter released a horse from the neighboring property. Valles was watching a similar scene, as neighbors used garden hoses to put out whatever they could—with photojournalist Joel Cooke continuing to pitch in. A resident named Mike Rodgers stood in the doorway of his home wearing a Chicago Bears beanie, his eyeglasses folded and hanging from his shirt. When Valles asked him what he needed, Rodgers looked across the street, hands on his hips, and paused.

"I could use a cup of coffee."

The home across the street was completely engulfed.

"We're just trying to save what we have."

"What made you come back home?" Valles asked about why the Rodgers family returned after having evacuated the night before.

"This is home, what are we going to do?" he replied. "Where are we going to go?"

A neighbor climbed onto his roof clutching a garden hose, silhouetted by the rising sun and smoke behind him. The water pressure was visibly low, though, a mere trickle coming out of the nozzle in his hand.

A rescue fire truck from Los Angeles County Station No. 111—dispatched from Valencia, a neighborhood in Santa Clarita, forty miles to the north—drove down the street without stopping, looking for the next place they could continue their fight as the wind shifted from the southwest to the northeast.

Mike and Jenny Rodgers crossed the street, doing what they could to fight the flames as they began to encroach on another house.

"Neighbors helping neighbors. Doing what they can," Valles said.

From my brother and sister-in-law's would-be future home, we started back toward our crew, but first I had another stop to make. Jake and Cara Levine had lived on El Medio, just above Pali High, and I took the exact same drive I had hundreds of times to their mom's place: left off Bienveneda to Sunset. Follow the winding curves just under a mile and a half to their turnoff.

The morning weather was similar, chilly and overcast, as so many of those carpool pickups were. Different this time were the downed power lines. The soaked streets from hydrants run dry. The fire trucks parked in the middle of Sunset. And the burning, still happening on both sides of the street.

At El Medio, we made a right, across from the shell of the church Sixty-Nines couldn't save. As we drove down the street, I remembered the sounds of the Dave Matthews Band, Barenaked Ladies, and Simon & Garfunkel that I would listen to until my passengers would make me put in a new CD (don't judge me). I never remembered the Levines' address because I knew the house. Didn't need to know the numbers. But as I rolled down the street, so many of them were gone that I could see all the way down into Temescal Canyon, where Pali High was, over the smoldering ruins of so many homes.

I tracked the numbers on the curb, and when I got close, I realized it wasn't looking good. I pulled up to their house, and on my left all that was left was a chimney, their mom's burned-out car, and pockets of smoke rising from remnants of their beautiful home. Palm fronds charred to a crisp lined the gutter in front of the house. Their neighbors' homes were gone, too. It was 7:47 a.m. I took a photo, but there was no cell service, so I turned around and drove back toward Sunset. The message went through at 7:54 a.m., when I had enough cell signal back at our broadcast location to get it through.

Levine was still inside the SCIF without his phone, which allowed his anxiety about what was happening in his hometown to fade to the background as he focused on optimistic feelings about his work on Ukraine, and, later in the day, tackling the process of closing out his work with the administration. At eleven o'clock Eastern time—8 a.m. in Los Angeles—Jake walked out of the secure room and with others went to the cabinet to grab his phone.

A colleague approached him with a question. Just then, he looked down to see my message.

> Call me
>
> House is gone. So sorry

Levine's mind went immediately blank.

"I'm so sorry. I have to go."

He left the White House at once, went home to pack his bag, and went to the airport to fly back to Los Angeles.

At almost the same time I was texting with him at the White

House, I received a call from a member of the incoming Trump administration. It was like seeing a ghost.

"Hello?"

"Hi, it's Katie Miller."

Or, as I first knew her, Katie Waldman—one of the lower-level spokespeople for the Department of Homeland Security during the first Trump administration. Waldman is *now* Katie Miller after marrying Stephen Miller, one of President Trump's most trusted aides and masterminds of his immigrant family separation policy. She had worked closely with me to allow access inside the detention centers to see the policy in action for myself when I covered it in 2018.

I was shocked. I could not believe I was hearing from her. I couldn't understand why. I wrote about her in my first book, and when the details of conversations we had about the policy—and her feelings about it—were published, she cut off all contact with me.

I'm not even sure if it fully registered that she was on the phone. The last time I had reached out to her, in March 2023, I never heard back. Now, I didn't have time to focus on what she might want.

I told her I had to call her back right as Lester Holt began an NBC News special report—breaking into local programming—to televise a news conference of local officials who were going to report on the latest details of the multiple blazes burning throughout Southern California.

Three notes in the key of G played into my earpiece—G, E, and C—to identify the National Broadcasting Company—the same chimes played since November 29, 1929.

"This is an NBC News special report," the announcer declared over the musical fanfare that signaled—especially to me as a kid growing up in the Palisades—something big was about to be announced. "Here's Lester Holt." We had been told to get in position to talk to Lester after the officials had wrapped up their remarks, so I stood at attention in front of the camera, back where the homes continued to burn on Pampas Ricas. Lester quickly threw to the news conference.

Anthony Marrone, the chief of the Los Angeles County Fire Department, surrounded by a phalanx of the city and county's top officials—save Karen Bass, Los Angeles's mayor, who was still en route back from Ghana—updated the latest statistics about the Palisades and Eaton Fires. Finger pointing had already begun about how the mayor could be absent given the warnings issued, and her office insisted (and continued to after the fires) the mayor herself was not aware of the level of danger the city faced because it was not communicated to her by Kristin Crowley, her fire chief, something Crowley later denied.

With Crowley by his side, Marrone said the Palisades Fire was "well over five thousand acres that have burned, and the fire is growing. We have no percentage of containment. We have an estimated one thousand structures destroyed. And also no reported fatalities and a high number of significant injuries to residents who did not evacuate in addition to first responders who were on the fire line." At the same time, a thousand personnel were still fighting the blaze.

The Eaton Fire had claimed over two thousand acres, he said, noting, "The fire continues to grow with zero percent containment. We have over five hundred personnel assigned, and, unfortunately, we have two reported fatalities to civilians—unknown cause at this time—and we do have a number of significant injuries. We have over a hundred structures destroyed, and the cause of the fire is unknown and under investigation."

As I listened, I couldn't get the call from Katie Miller out of my head.

What does she want?

I looked down at my phone to see a text message from her. She was asking if I knew whether a specific street in the Palisades had burned down. Then she sent an address. I couldn't imagine whose it might be. But I had to focus on what officials were saying, and what I was about to say on national television.

As Los Angeles officials held their press conference, Jake Torres and the Los Angeles County firefighters of Nineteens rolled back up to Loma Alta Drive and Fair Oaks Avenue in Altadena, where they had responded to a wires-down call at three o'clock the previous day, before the Eaton Fire broke out. Torres's engine needed gas, and they were in the area to top off the tank.

When he was here last, the intersection was a mess, with utility poles and wires blocking the way until they were able to secure them. Another firefighter on the engine stopped him because she noticed that they were back where they had been the day prior.

"Do you remember being on the wires down on this corner yesterday?"

Torres realized where they were. But instead of pine trees and the corner park and the small, beautiful homes with the bus stop off to the side, there was nothing. Everything had burned. His fight-or-flight adrenaline still pumping, he allowed himself a moment to absorb what had happened.

Oh my God.

As they continued through the neighborhood, every single house for what seemed like a mile was on fire.

Even if we have all the water in the world, we're not stopping that.

But Nineteens kept going, rolling through Altadena to look for any human or structure they could save.

* * *

For around twenty minutes, I stood ready to join Lester, listening to official after official come to the podium. But I could not stop thinking about the address Katie Miller sent, and who it belonged to.

Stephen Miller, her husband, grew up in Santa Monica, just down Pacific Coast Highway from the Palisades. Katie, who went on to become Vice President Mike Pence's spokesperson before publicly falling out with him in the wake of the January 6, 2021, attack on the US Capitol, had been announced in late December as an incoming administration staff member at Elon Musk's stated effort to slash waste from the government. "Katie Miller will soon be joining DOGE!" President-elect Trump wrote. "She has been a loyal supporter of mine for many years, and will bring her professional experience to Government Efficiency."

As I waited to join Lester, I wrote back.

"Sorry to hang up so fast about to go up on a special report will call you after I get over there," I texted.

"It's Stephen's parents' house. Thank you so much," she wrote back. "You're the only one who I can see is there. They are desperate to know."

Is this really happening? Am I being asked to go to Stephen Miller's parents' house?

I was.

"I'll find out. Been doing for others too. My brother's house about to burn down," I said.

"So sad." She asked if most of the streets around where she told me the Millers' home was had burned.

"Yes most . . . gone."

"When do you think you'd get to theirs. They are hopeful but I think unlikely. Thanks so much. It's so terrible. It's their whole life."

I could not believe it. But I didn't have time to process. I joined Lester on the special report, this time with my mask and goggles both on, as the wind had shifted again, and choking smoke was making it hard to breathe—or even to see as it infiltrated my goggles. After I gave Lester, who spends a considerable amount of time in Los Angeles and is from Northern California, the state of play on the ground, he added his own view of what was playing out across the country from the studio he sat in.

"Yeah, Jacob, I have been covering wildfires in Northern and Southern California since the earliest days of my career, going back into the late seventies. I have never seen anything like this. Do you agree?"

"There's no doubt about it. LA is a city of communities, Lester—you know this as well as anyone from the time that you have spent here. And Pacific Palisades is one of those communities. Pacific Palisades, for all intents and purposes, has been wiped off the map as we know it."

Lester thanked me, and I took out my earpiece. I couldn't stop thinking about what Katie Miller had called about. So I drove to Stephen Miller's parents' house almost immediately, pulling up in front of their home at 8:37 a.m. There was nothing left. Homes up and down the block had burned down, including the Millers'.

Their black automatic gate had been left open. Only the three-foot wall covered with vines and the numbers marking their address was left, along with some of the succulents planted on the curb. I could see clear through several blocks toward Sunset. There was nothing but two steel beams that rose from the rubble of the home. Whatever it looked like two days prior, I had no idea. I sent her an image, just as I had to Jake Levine, followed by several messages.

[Whole] neighborhood is gone

I'm sorry

> Seriously if any message you want me to convey from PEOTUS lmk
>
> Sorry you're going through this

PEOTUS, President Elect of the United States.

"I am so sad for them," she replied.

"Me too. Sorry again."

"Thank you for going there."

"Palisades is stronger than politics in my book," I wrote, with the belief that our at times adversarial journalist-source relationship could be set aside, at least in the moment. I added a red heart emoji.

This is all so surreal, I thought to myself. For a moment, I'd considered not reaching out further—but the moment called for an olive branch. Maybe it was her offering me one?

I decided to call her, and did on FaceTime at eight forty-five in the morning as I drove down Chautauqua toward a facility on the beach that was doubling as the makeshift gas station Tim Larson from Twenty-Threes filled up at overnight. Katie picked up. She had the flu, she told me. We talked a little about Stephen's parents, and their invaluable sentimental possessions that were in the house, including paintings by his grandmother. I found myself feeling awful for them, and her family. We were all going through something similarly gutting—losing so much of what makes us who we are.

The call lasted less than a minute, and we hung up after expressing the same sympathies we had over text. For a minute, it felt as though our bad blood had been left aside.

We had that conversation before I saw what, minutes before she and I had FaceTimed, her once-and-future boss sent out as his first message about the fires on his social media platform. It was a message filled with misinformation about the cause of the fires and what Trump said was a potential solution to it.

> Governor Gavin Newscum refused to sign the water restoration declaration put before him that would have allowed millions of gallons of water, from excess rain and snow melt from the North, to flow daily into many parts of California, including the areas that are currently burning in a virtually apocalyptic way. He wanted to protect an essentially worthless fish called a smelt, by giving it less water (it didn't work!), but didn't care about the people of California. Now the ultimate price is being paid. I will demand that this incompetent governor allow beautiful, clean, fresh water to FLOW INTO CALIFORNIA! He is the blame for this. On top of it all, no water for fire hydrants, not firefighting planes. A true disaster!

At 8:53 a.m., Katie Miller's current boss, Elon Musk, shared it to his hundreds of millions of followers on X, a post reshared over fifty thousand times and seen by as many as thirty-eight million people. I wondered if he knew about the Millers' home. None of the misinformation he was sharing would have saved it. Instead, it would seep into the collective consciousness of people across the world like the toxins that were seeping into the bodies of so many of us in the Palisades and Altadena.

16

"It's Gone, Dad"

AT THE INTERSECTION OF MIDWICK DRIVE AND SINALOA Avenue in Altadena, neighbors had mobilized to stop a situation almost exactly the same as I had seen playing out across the street from my brother's home in the Palisades. Flames from a house, fully engulfed, were pouring up and over the fence toward the home of Eric Fiedler and his son Christopher, which had survived the fire that night. With two garden hoses and a ladder, they climbed to the roof to attempt to beat back the flames by wetting the roof and the hedges. It was 9:25 a.m.

One resident who was wearing a cutoff black T-shirt and sunglasses used the shirt to cover his mouth to prevent smoke from asphyxiating him. A fire truck from Riverside County Cal Fire pulled up, resulting in the exalted screams of even the KNBC reporter on the scene, Michelle Valles.

"Thank you so much! Oh, my goodness. Praise the Lord."

Around the same time the Riverside County firefighters battled the flames on Sinaloa, Ashley, the daughter of Herb and Loyda Wilson, was heading back toward their house two miles away after evacuating for the night to see if McNally Avenue had survived. By the time she and her boyfriend got close, she knew it wasn't good. She called her parents, in Hawaii, inconsolable.

"It's gone, Dad! Everything is gone!"

"Relax," Herb told his daughter in the Hawaiian darkness. "It's going to be OK."

Cate Heneghan had been receiving reports from her neighbors, too. One of them, who grew up in the home she still lived in on McNally Avenue, had tried to get close around six in the morning. But she told Cate that when she drove past Fairoaks Burger, less than a tenth of a mile away and just around the corner, all she saw was flames.

Cate attempted to get back to the block as well, but when she was within a half mile, she thought better of it.

I don't want to be part of the problem. I know it's gone. It's gone, Cate. Just let it go.

Even though she saw homes just a few blocks away that were still standing, her gut told her to turn around, so she did.

Nick Schuler of Cal Fire, the state fire agency, had a thought run through his head he had never experienced in all of his years of fighting fires.

God, I hope I don't die of cancer. This is not a good place to be. Thousands of homes have burned.

He was in the smoldering heart of the Palisades. He and Governor Newsom were driving through the area after a morning fire briefing, trying to find a cell signal for Newsom to reach President Biden. *My damn cell phone*, the governor thought. He had initiated the call because he was going to elevate the asks about resources, personnel, equipment, and federal reimbursements for what people were already saying could potentially be the costliest natural disaster in American history.

As the fire continued to rage both in the neighborhoods and on the ridges of the Santa Monica Mountains, the governor directed his security detail to pull over.

"Guys, turn left. Just stop. Stop."

He checked the bars on his cell phone.

"No. Jesus Christ."

He couldn't get a signal.

"You know, get near the gas station—it worked there last night."

At 9:41 a.m. we came across Governor Newsom and Schuler outside that gas station. Newsom had declared a state of emergency on Tuesday after the Palisades Fire broke out, and with it deployed hundreds of members of the California National Guard to Los Angeles. Once the Eaton Fire ignited, he knew that a major disaster declaration was needed—and had to be requested of President Biden, who was still in town—in order to mobilize federal resources for the Palisades, Eaton, Hurst, and Woodley Fires, now burning. The Hurst Fire had broken out Tuesday night and was growing in size in the north San Fernando Valley, surpassing five hundred acres Wednesday morning. Smoke plumes were rising from all corners of Los Angeles County. The Woodley fire started early Wednesday, a few dozen acre blaze in the Sepulveda Basin.

Like Schuler, I, too, was aware but perhaps not so acutely that our surroundings were not good for our health. My head was pounding. But I wanted to see my house and the rest of my community to understand, in the light of day, what was left and what wasn't. As we drove past the 76 gas station at Via de la Paz and Sunset, I saw multiple black SUVs with flashing lights on the side of the road, across from what used to be Jacopo's Pizza—burned to the ground—and directly next to the Gelson's supermarket, also gone. Tactical agents with long rifles were standing next to the motorcade. I knew the president was in town, but I assumed it was Governor Newsom because of the size of the detail. We pulled over, and I got out and walked toward the vehicles.

The governor, sitting in the right rear passenger seat, had his window cracked open, and a phone pressed to his ear. I had interviewed or run into Newsom multiple times—during the failed recall effort against him in 2021, on the floor of the 2024 Democratic National Convention in Chicago, and elsewhere—and he had told me he followed my reporting on immigration closely during the first Trump term. I felt comfortable approaching the car—something his advance team, staff, and guys with long rifles didn't seem to appreciate.

The governor and I made eye contact. Holding his hand over the receiver and pointing to the phone, he mouthed to me, "I'm talking to Biden. I can't talk." I can be pushy, but I knew enough to walk away, giving him the space to speak with the president. I hoped for an interview when he was off the phone.

It was a bit of a fib by Newsom. He hadn't yet gotten through.

"Sir, one moment for the president," the White House operator eventually said to Newsom as his signal kept going in and out. While he attempted to reach Biden, I spoke to Schuler in the gas station parking lot.

"In my twenty-six years, this could be one of the top, most devastating fires I've seen," he said.

"What happens in a situation like this?" I wanted to know. "The high school is destroyed. You've got churches destroyed. The two supermarkets in the community destroyed. How do you come back from something like this?"

"You come back one day at a time," Schuler told me.

When Newsom's signal continued to drop, he was driven around the corner to attempt to reach the president yet again.

"They're gonna think I'm an asshole," Newsom griped to an aide about leaving me and the crew behind.

With a satellite phone, Newsom tried again to reach Biden, and, feeling panicked because it was not working, he got out of the car and walked the streets searching for a cell signal. Confronted by a frantic local resident, Newsom explained what he was trying to do.

"I'm literally talking to the president right now to specifically answer the question of what we can do for you and your daughter."

"Can I hear it?" the woman asked.

Newsom, pointing to his cell phone service bars, told her about the trouble he was having connecting.

"There's literally—I've tried five times. That's why I'm walking around to make the call."

Newsom got back into his SUV. At 9:49 a.m. the White House pool reporter sent out a dispatch: "The president spoke with California Governor Gavin Newsom by phone to receive the latest update on the wildfires across Los Angeles." They planned to meet less than an hour later, where Newsom would hand-deliver the disaster declaration request to Biden.

Meanwhile, as Los Angeles County Twelves continued to fight on the western flank of the Eaton Fire, hydrants started to go dry. The flames had not only overtaken McNally Avenue but also spread even farther toward Pasadena, where the Rose Bowl was now the active incident command post. By 10 a.m., Captain Joshua Swaney realized that the hydrants were dead, requiring runs to Pasadena to fill up their water tank and return to the blaze. At the Pasadena Convention Center, residents lined the walls and slumped on the floors. Wheelchairs and stretchers were visible down the hallway. KNBC was covering it live.

Going to Pasadena and the command post for relief wasn't in the cards for Twelves, whose members' heads were throbbing and eyes were bloodshot. They were subsisting on old military

MREs—meals ready to eat—stashed in the truck, along with energy bars and whatever drinking water they had. County policy requires that fire engines need to be self-sustaining for three days, a function of being so close to so many potential massive brush fires in the San Gabriels. But this was another order of magnitude—a full-scale urban conflagration.

While in the Palisades the sun and some blue sky continued randomly to break through, Altadena remained under a shroud of greyness at the intersection of El Molino Avenue and Sacramento Street. Lemons and oranges hung off the trees at the height of citrus season. A loud explosion boomed as they had continued from one end of Los Angeles County in the Palisades to the other in Altadena for nearly twenty-four hours. The din caused another veteran reporter, KNBC's Conan Nolan, to question was happening around him, realizing he had no idea.

Still behind the wheel, I rolled up to my childhood home on Frontera Drive in the Palisades around 10:20 a.m. Even before we turned the corner, I could visualize its ruins. I was right.

On the way there, I had run into two guys on bikes who had snuck back into the Palisades around the checkpoints set up by the Los Angeles Police Department. If it wasn't for the blue KN95 masks hanging off their ears, they could be on a regular morning ride through the neighborhood. I pulled over to them and rolled down the window. They were going through the same stage of grief as I was.

"I know my house is gone," one of them said, "but I just need to see it firsthand to let it set in. I just can't believe it."

"I thought I was going to wake up this morning, and it was going to be a bad dream," said the other. I told them to be safe and pulled away.

When I got to our old house, I opened the door of the Wagoneer and swung my legs out. A fire engine sat outside—but there was nothing to save.

"I don't really know what to say" were the words that came out as our crew filmed me in real time. My hands were thrust in the pockets of my green fire pants, my NBC News baseball hat was on, and my face was caked in the soot we had been standing in all morning. The house was made of red brick, later painted white by the owner who bought it from my parents when I was around five or six. But when the house collapsed, the red brick was exposed again, as if the house were opening up to reveal something I hadn't seen since we moved away. Welcoming me back home. I remember standing on the same street corner manning a lemonade stand with my brother. And hanging in our backyard pool with my sisters. And looking out my bedroom window at the street. There was nothing left.

I pulled out my phone and called my mom on FaceTime.

"Mom? Look at this."

"Is that Frontera? Your birth house?" she asked as I panned the camera across the landscape, which looked as if it could have taken a direct hit from a ballistic missile—not all that different from what I had seen on the outskirts of Lviv, Ukraine, covering the early weeks of the war there.

"Yup."

My mom let out a noise that was somewhere between a whimper and a sob.

"I'm so sad," she said. "Every one of you was born in that house."

The wind was picking up, and it was hard to hear her, but the devastated look on her face communicated volumes.

"I know. It makes me—it makes me sad, too," I told her, choking back tears of my own. We talked for a while, and then I hung up. Tears traced a line through the blackness on my cheeks.

Eventually, standing on the sidewalk in front of the same white picket fence—now a dirty shade of grey entangled with the rose bushes that had butted up against them for decades—I got it together enough to look directly into the camera and reflect, for the first time, on what was really just beginning, for a report that would air on *NBC Nightly News* later that evening.

"This was a really, really special place for the Soboroff family. And I'm very sorry to see it go. And I'm very sorry for all of the residents of Pacific Palisades and everyone across the greater LA area that's going through this right now. I look around the town, the neighborhood, the place that I grew up in. I talk to my friends who I spent so much time with on these streets, and it's hard to imagine what comes next and what happens next."

And then we went back to work.

17

"It's Astounding"

PRESIDENT JOE BIDEN PULLED UP TO TO SANTA MONICA'S FIRE STAtion No. 5 after leaving Cedars-Sinai Medical Center, near Beverly Hills, where he spent less than an hour at the scheduled C-section birth of his first great-grandchild. A boy, named William Brannon Neal, IV, was born to his granddaughter Naomi and son-in-law Peter Neal. On the fifteen-minute-long drive a "huge, billowing smoke cloud" was visible as they headed toward the Palisades Fire, pooler Danny Kemp of Agence France-Presse reported about their drive westward on the Santa Monica freeway.

Governor Gavin Newsom, who was waiting for Biden at the fire station, had one mission for the event: get the president to agree to approve a major disaster declaration. Normally, it is a massive document that details how and why the scale and scope of destruction require federal government assistance and reimbursement. But Newsom had time to put together only two pages, which he had printed out and carried with him into a hallway where he met face-to-face with the president twenty-four hours after they were first scheduled to meet to declare the two new national monuments in the Southern California desert.

"Mr. President, here's the official request," Newsom said to Biden, handing him the crumpled paperwork that would jump-start the recovery process for the now multiple fires—not just the two massive ones—burning in the Los Angeles area, even as zero percent of them had been contained. It read:

> Dear Mr. President,
>
> This letter serves as my request for a Major Disaster Declaration related to the conditions in Southern California due to the Palisades, Eaton, Franklin [which had burned Malibu the prior month] and Hurst wildfires and ongoing windstorm event, including subsequent wildfires that may erupt under the current hazardous conditions (collectively January Wildfires and Windstorm event), which commenced January 7, 2025, and continue to overwhelm Los Angeles County due to the complex nature of the ongoing fires and dangerous windstorm conditions continuing to pose a further threat to the county and its residents. To date, over 1,000 structures, including residences, have been destroyed, with over 110,000 residents under mandatory evacuation orders, placing a strain on resources available to respond to the fires.
>
> As such, under the provisions of Section 401 of the Robert T. Stafford Disaster Relief and Emergency Assistance Act, 42 U.S.C. §§ 5121–5207 (Stafford Act), as implemented by 44 C.F.R. § 206.36, I respectfully request an emergency Major Disaster Declaration for Los Angeles County, to include:
>
> - All categories of Public Assistance;
> - All Individual Assistance programs;

- Any other appropriate Stafford Act disaster assistance programs;

- US Small Business Administration disaster loans and funds from the US Department of Agriculture Emergency Loan Program; and

- Hazard Mitigation statewide.

Thank you for your consideration and your continued support for the State of California.

Sincerely
Gavin Newsom

Governor of California

Newsom's name was signed hastily in blue ink, his signature scratching through his own printed name on the flimsy page.

"Pal," Biden said to Newsom, "done."

Biden and Newsom, joined by California senator Alex Padilla and other local officials, walked out to brief the press on the apparatus floor where the engines would normally sit, now deployed to fight the Palisades Fire in a mutual-aid effort.

"Well, the governor asked for a declaration that provides for everything the federal government can do, and I'm prepared to sign it today," Biden said at the start of his remarks. "The—it's going to take time. But we're in it. The federal government is here to stay as long as you need us and everything you need."

When he concluded, Newsom thanked him.

"On behalf of all of us, Mr. President, thank you for being here—and not just being here today. Thank you for being here since the minute of this incident when it was a ten-acre fire less than twenty-four or so hours ago. My deep gratitude."

"It's astounding what's happened," the president replied.

Within minutes of the press availability concluding, President-elect Trump took to Truth Social, his social media site, and fired off an all-caps message:

> NO WATER IN THE FIRE HYDRANTS, NO MONEY IN FEMA. THIS IS WHAT JOE BIDEN IS LEAVING ME. THANKS JOE!

A half hour later, another:

> The fires in Los Angeles may go down, in dollar amount, as the worst in the History of our Country. In many circles, they're doubting whether insurance companies will even have enough money to pay for this catastrophe. Let this serve, and be emblematic, of the gross incompetence and mismanagement of the Biden/Newscum Duo. January 20th cannot come fast enough!

While President-elect Trump was blaming the fire on "gross incompetence and mismanagement," I was standing at the improvised gas station on the Pacific Coast Highway. I was joining my friend Katy Tur—a fellow native Palisadian—on her MSNBC broadcast. My eyes were watering as I held my hand to my earpiece to hear Katy recount her memories of growing up in the Palisades from the studio at 30 Rock.

"So many people that we love and grew up with have lost everything," she said before throwing to me just as a fire engine from Manhattan Beach pulled up behind me.

I told her that where I was standing was "a great way to understand that this is a mutual-aid environment. This is an impromptu gas station, and so all the different agencies—come and look at this," I told cameraman Alan Rice as we walked toward the driver's-side door of Manhattan Beach's Engine Company No. 21—"through all of Southern California are coming here to fuel up their fire trucks before they go back out into service."

I looked up, and sitting in the driver's seat was an engineer whose face was covered in soot. His arm was draped outside of the window as if to let it relax only for a moment.

"Thank you for doing this—really appreciate it," I said to him. "Manhattan Beach?"

He nodded yes.

"Can I just ask you real quick: Have you ever seen anything like this before?" I angled the stick mic toward him.

"I've seen it one more time; I've seen it before at the Woolsey," he said of the deadly 2018 Ventura County fire.

"How you doing? You feeling OK?" I asked.

"Yeah, we're hanging in there. We've been up for over twenty-four hours."

What he didn't tell me was that he and his company had been toiling to save property and lives at the bottom of Palisades Drive when the flames from the Highlands quickly raced down toward the ocean at the very beginning of the firefight. He was there when the bulldozer plowed through, making way for his engine and others to continue into the Palisades.

"You going to get any rest anytime soon?"

"Not until . . . hopefully, tomorrow."

He flashed me a thumbs-up.

"God bless you. What's your name?"

"James."

"James, I'm Jacob."

James was James Stratton, the veteran engineer who'd told his captain to shoot the header as they raced toward the fire twenty-four hours ago. It was around then they saw the Super Scooper aircraft dipping into the Pacific Ocean to grab water to attack the flames they were now sitting next to as they fueled their tank.

With his right hand, he reached across his body and we shook hands. I touched the letters spelling *Manhattan* on his driver's-side door.

"Thank you, nice to meet you."

Still on the air, I walked away from the truck as the wind picked up again and nearly blew my hat off. I had something I wanted to say to Katy.

"You and I . . . I think the viewers of your program know we have been friends for a very long time. And you and I would drive around in my old Prius through the streets of Pacific Palisades together when we were sixteen, seventeen years old. You don't recognize what's going on there anymore. It doesn't look like the Pacific Palisades that you and I know. And I can't wait for you to come out here and, honestly"—my voice cracked—"to give you a big hug and for you to give a big hug to a lot of people who love you very much and I know you love."

We completed our report, during which President Biden took off on Air Force One for Washington, and I returned to the Wagoneer, devouring whatever was left of our energy bars and Coke Zeros. Then we made a U-turn on PCH and climbed back up Chautauqua into the Palisades, where Mayor Karen Bass, back home after being absent from her own city before and as the fires broke out despite clear warnings of potential catastrophe received by city officials, joined Governor Newsom and Senator Padilla on a walking tour. Hours earlier, as she deplaned at Los Angeles International Airport, Bass stared blankly without commenting as Sky News reporter David Blevins bird-dogged her about the fires and her leadership. Padilla stopped to take pictures of the devastation all around them.

By one o'clock on day two of the Great Los Angeles Fires, the Palisades Fire had consumed more than 11,800 acres; the Eaton Fire, more than 10,600 acres; the smaller Hurst Fire, over 500 acres; and the latecomer, the Woodley Fire in the San Fernando Valley's Sepulveda Basin, 30 acres. Over a thousand structures had been destroyed by the Palisades Fire alone. And so many others were still burning.

Back in the heart of the Palisades, we continued to survey the devastation on streets we had not yet visited, and looked for another location from which to broadcast live. As we drove through the neighborhood on the beach side of Sunset just south of my old synagogue, we came upon a young man who told us his name was James. There were just over fifteen minutes until we needed to establish a strong signal with our portable satellite and get on the air for Nicolle Wallace's afternoon program on MSNBC. James was wearing a blue T-shirt with the yellow logo of the annual Griffith Park Trail Marathon Relay and 8K race.

In 1933 Griffith Park had been the location—before the Camp Fire in Paradise killed eighty-five people in 2018—of the single deadliest wildfire in California history, a tragedy that killed at least twenty-nine workers who were part of a nearly four-thousand-person crew hired to clear brush and build roads as part of a public works project to get people back to work during the Great Depression. It was hard not to wonder how the fires burning throughout Los Angeles would compare to the devastation and lethality of the infamous Griffith Park blaze.

But James wasn't thinking about any of that. He had ridden his bicycle, wearing safety goggles like you'd find in a high school science lab, and an industrial-grade respirator with two pink canisters attached, as he attempted to put out spot fires at what I assumed was his house when homes just down the block were engulfed.

"Can you please text my mom and dad to let them know I'm OK and our house is still standing?" he screamed to me as the wind whipped his brown hair. "Their names are Bob and Mimi Kahn."

I took their number and did.

> Bob and Mimi. This is Jacob Soboroff from NBC News. James wants you to know the house is ok and he's safe. He just doesn't have cell service.

"Thank you so much," his father texted back.

"Oh my! Thank you," Mimi wrote. "All of our neighbors are asking about their homes. What does Wildomar and junaluska look like near our house?"

I didn't have time to text back—or to tell them I was worried about James's safety, as he was using a small hand shovel to pick up and stomp out embers on and around the property. We moved down the block, where the smoke was so thick—the fires still burning homes that hadn't been flattened and igniting new ones at the same time—that I put on my goggles over my backward hat and crisscrossed the yellow rubber bands of my N95 mask as tight as possible. As Nicolle Wallace brought me into her program, I looked over my left shoulder as a gust of wind thrust me backward—a wind as strong as any I had felt since the night before.

"This is nowhere near from being over," I told her, the lines between an extended attack—the process of drawing up more forces and firefighting resources to stabilize what was still unfolding and an initial attack feeling blurred by the black smoke that was swirling. "Everywhere you look, this inferno continues to grow." It was one o'clock in the afternoon, but the sky was darkening yet again.

"It is . . . it is . . . it is . . . unimaginable to see it in this state," I said of my hometown. As I waved my hands around for emphasis, you could see my palms covered in black soot.

"I remember as a kid my parents packed up the car and drove us out of the neighborhood because we were worried about a wildfire. Never, ever has it turned into something like this."

Nicolle asked what it was like to be there covering the fires.

"As far as being a reporter here, we're here to do our jobs. But I do have to say I have never quite experienced something so personal in such a way as this. This is not about me, but there's a small part of me that feels what these people are going through tonight. I saw my childhood home that I had grown up in," I told her, "and it had burned down as well."

We lost our signal in the middle of the report. Before we got in the cars to leave the neighborhood, we noticed the building that had just ignited—a garage kitty-corner from where we were reporting—was now a total loss. As we left, we bid goodbye to James Kahn. He wouldn't budge—and I worried if he'd make it out alive.

Gavin Newsom was en route to the Eaton Fire when he received news he had been waiting for: President Biden formally declared the major disaster declaration for the Los Angeles Fires. Twelve minutes later, the governor was at the command post at the Rose Bowl, receiving a briefing about the fire. From there, he went to Altadena, landing just after three o'clock smack in between Fire Station No. 12 and the block of McNally Avenue where Loyda and Herb Wilson hoped to get to from Hawaii as soon as possible.

It looked like dusk, but sunset was still hours away. The homes on the block were gone, but fires were still burning behind cars and from piles of rubble. Newsom, not wearing a mask, was speaking to Alex Padilla, his voice sounding more gravelly than usual. So did everyone else. Nick Schuler, the Cal Fire veteran, stared off into the debris in front of him. His mother had grown up in Altadena, and he had never been to see her childhood home. Now he never would. It had burned down—a reminder of how lucky he was.

This could have been my community. There are so many people that are going to be in a difficult place for years.

For Schuler and the rest of the more than 7,500 firefighting and emergency personnel deployed to this disaster, the transition to an extended attack was underway.

Long-term planning would need to get jumpstarted immediately, even as the fire was burning all across Los Angeles County. But a local fire this was not, the governor realized. This was something bigger, with more to come. And in just twelve days, Donald Trump, whose only public response to the fires was to cast blame and sow disinformation, would become president of the United States for a second time.

18

"Oh No"

AS GOVERNOR NEWSOM WAS ARRIVING IN ALTADENA, I had pulled up to Via de la Paz, a main commercial tributary in the Palisades village off Sunset. The street name means Way of Peace in Spanish, so named by the Methodist founders of Pacific Palisades in the 1920s. A Methodist church still sat on Via de la Paz, although when we pulled up, much of it had already burned and more would burn yet. The winds were blowing now from the center of the village out toward the bluffs where the early Palisades Methodists would hold Easter services on what they called Peace Hill. Just when I thought I might see another sliver of blue sky—the winds having swatted away the smoke for a fleeting moment—a massive cloud of grey haze rolled in.

I had a message for people who were calling and texting, continuing to ask me to go by their homes: "Pacific Palisades as you know it is gone." Nicolle Wallace, who I had rejoined on air, let out a sigh and, a moment later, asked me what that meant.

"I was just saying to Bianca," our producer, "that right down this street—I'll just show you—there's a veterinarian's office. My parents were animal people and had a lot of dogs over the course of our childhood. That was our vet!" I said, pointing to a brick building on the left. "That was my pediatrician's office, Nicolle." I pointed to the opposite corner, almost excited to remember what once stood there. It was like my eyes had an overlay from Google Street View, or my own memories, and I could see it all. "If you make a right-hand turn, there's a restaurant—or was one—Café Vida, and next to that was the Chinese restaurant, Cathay Palisades, and next to that was the local Starbucks."

Nicolle thanked me for the report—but before I wrapped up, I asked her if I could share one more thing.

"There are a lot of people who come and work and support the people who live in these communities and the homes and the businesses that keep them open. They're not the residents. But they're the people from other parts of Los Angeles—maybe not as affluent or as in the spotlight, but Pacific Palisades doesn't just run on Palisadians." A smile—the first I'd felt in over twenty-four hours—started to stretch across my filthy face as I remembered people like Albino Fuentes, or Albie, who worked at Café Vida and before that Mort's Deli around the corner. "It runs on Angelenos—people from all over this city that come here and make it what it is. I hope everybody can hold a little something in their heart for all those people tonight, too. Because this is a community that is as much theirs as the people who lay their head here at night." I finished while holding my hand to my heart as a fireball exploded inside a two-story building over my right shoulder.

I stood in that same spot reporting for the next three hours—for hosts Ari Melber, Joy Reid, and, finally, for Chris Hayes during the five o'clock local hour. Before getting out of the car to report one last time, the Methodist church completely burned to the ground. I snapped a somber selfie to send to my family. Wrinkles I had never seen in my face were visible. My cheeks were red. My eyes were bloodshot and half open. I looked like what I imagined H. G. Wells's Time Traveller did when seeing a world he could have never imagined: "dusty and dirty, and smeared with green down the sleeves; his hair disordered, and as it seemed to me greyer—either with dust and dirt or because its colour had actually faded. His face was ghastly pale; his chin had a brown cut on it—a cut half-healed; his expression was haggard and drawn, as by intense suffering." I felt like I had lived a lifetime in just one day.

Chris Hayes asked me to confirm what he had been hearing—that nobody in Los Angeles had ever seen anything like what we were experiencing in real time.

"It's sickening, is how I would describe it, Chris." My head was pounding, despite my having taken the medication I always keep on hand as a sufferer of migraines.

I was holding the microphone with my right hand, my thumb pressed up against the bottom of the microphone itself and my other four fingers tightly wrapped around the stick. My wife, watching the news with my parents and children, having evacuated from our home in-between the two fires, took a video, zooming in on my hands which looked as if I had rubbed them in the discarded charcoal of a backyard barbecue.

"I think that's a fire," my four-year-old observed, watching her dad on TV. Within twenty minutes of her saying that, another fire had erupted in Los Angeles—this one near the same part of the Santa Monica Mountains where the Griffith Park Fire burned in 1933. Above Sunset Boulevard in the Santa Monica Mountains, they called it the Sunset Fire. I got into the Wagoneer and started driving home, grateful for whatever amount of sleep I could get before going back to work in the morning. But on the way, I noticed, from the darkness of the Santa Monica Freeway headed eastbound, fire in the mountains near the landmark Hollywood Sign to my left.

* * *

At 5:59 p.m. Los Angeles Fire Department Chief Kristin Crowley—from a press conference held in the city's Emergency Operations Center—texted the chiefs of the fire departments of Los Angeles County, Ventura County, and Orange County with yet more daunting news:

"Hollywood Hills brush fire. Anything you can send us. I'll send you a staging location."

The location came through thirty seconds later.

"Staging Sunset and Laurel Canyon."

"Oh no," texted Dustin Gardner from Ventura County. "Let me see what else we can pull."

Brian Hennessy from Orange County said he could "send 2–3 engine strike teams. Let me confirm."

Anthony Marrone, from LA County, had been part of the same press conference. He left at once to mobilize air support—which had been able to get back into the skies after having been grounded the night before—to the Hollywood Hills, now dubbed the Sunset Fire.

"I hope you two are doing OK," Gardner texted his colleagues later that night. "What a tough couple of days."

Flying from Hawaii to the Hollywood Burbank Airport, Loyda Wilson was in a window seat on the second of two connecting flights, and as the plane approached, she could see fire—now five fires—burning. Her husband, Herb, would follow her home later that night after staying behind to return their rental car to an off-airport location that wasn't open early enough for both of them to catch the same flight.

Unreal. Just unreal. My whole neighborhood is on fire. Those are the mountains right there.

When she landed, around 6 p.m., her daughter Ashley was waiting for her at the small airport.

"Let's go to the house. Let's go to the house."

"Mommy, they're not going to let you."

"I don't care, let's go."

They drove east toward Altadena. On their right side, the Sunset Fire was attempting to burn up and over and through homes in the Hollywood Hills, on the other side of the mountain.

With President Biden now back in Washington, KNBC was able to deploy its chopper and overlay the inferno with a street map that showed how the fire was centered around Runyon Canyon Road, a popular hiking spot for locals.

"I cannot emphasize strongly enough the need for everyone to follow our immediate evacuation orders," a Los Angeles City Fire Department representative said, calling into the station. Both the Palisades and Eaton Fires had exploded so fast. The systems meant to efficiently warn residents to evacuate failed to operate as intended, resulting in enormous confusion about evacuations, and she was now crystal clear that the Hollywood Hills needed to empty out as quickly as possible. The choppers that had been sent as a part of the mutual-aid effort kicked off by the local fire chiefs texting one another were engaged in water drops visible on live television.

When Gavin Newsom was made aware of the Sunset Fire, it felt like yet another body blow from the pounding relentlessness of the back-to-back-to-back-to-back fires. If there was any silver lining, the wind speeds had dropped and were calm where the Sunset Fire was burning, allowing for the aggressive firefighting effort now underway in the Hollywood Hills. The governor and his team made the decision to go the following morning to provide space for the battle—approaching dozens of acres—to take place and not interfere.

All of this was going on as Ashley and Loyda drove past. When they made it the twenty miles from Burbank Airport to Altadena,

Loyda saw from the ground what she had seen an hour or so earlier from the air. So much smoke. Such a haunting glow. Sirens. Cars. Commotion. They got all the way to Woodbury Drive and Lake Avenue. By then, reports indicated at least five were dead in their hometown and hundreds of structures were destroyed, including the historic Andrew McNally House nearby. Both counts were sure to rise.

"Mommy, we're not going to make it through."

Loyda was tired and devastated; she couldn't bring herself to get out of the car and walk—or even think to drive down Woodbury to be within a half mile of the house on McNally. They returned to Ashley's place in Pasadena until Herb would land later that night.

By Wednesday evening, the Eaton Fire had grown to over 10,600 acres; the Palisades Fire, over 15,000 acres; and the Sunset Fire was approaching 50 acres. At 8:40 p.m. local time, President-elect Trump sent out another message on social media:

> One of the best and most beautiful parts of the United States of America is burning down to the ground. It's ashes, and Gavin Newscum should resign. This is all his fault!!!

Trump's postings stopped the governor of the most populous state in the country on a dime. Newsom had a long-standing relationship with Trump—stretching back to when he was governor-elect and toured the aftermath of the Camp Fire in Paradise with Trump and then-governor Jerry Brown. During Trump's first term, Newsom had personally called the forty-fifth president regarding emergencies. Newsom would be the first to say that asking for help wasn't always easy with Trump, and needed a type of schmoozing and adulation that Trump seemed to require, but ultimately politics were always set aside to focus on recoveries—including during COVID. Newsom wasn't so sure tonight. Watching the series of attacks from Trump, he was taken aback, he later explained to me.

Who's this guy? You're still in campaign mode. You're the president of the United States. This is a different moment. An American moment.

The strange-bedfellows relationship that Newsom believed he had with Trump seemed to be gone. He wondered why he felt so . . . stung.

Was it naiveté?

The mis-and-disinformation Trump was spreading about the fires was making its way to even Governor Newsom's closest friends and family. Newsom was perplexed. Worn down. At the end of his rope. How could anyone possibly believe Trump's preposterous claims that Newsom was withholding (nonexistent) sources of "beautiful, clean, fresh water" from his own citizens? The thoughts raced through his head.

Where the hell are you getting this? How and why are they buying that same bullshit that's coming out of Fox and Newsmax and One America News—the sewage coming out of X? We're still in the middle of fighting multiple fires. Not one damn fire. Multiple fires.

The stress Newsom felt was piling up during what he saw as an opportunistic attempt by the president-elect to weaken his authority.

Loyda Wilson headed back to Burbank to pick up her husband, Herb, around eleven thirty at night. He hadn't slept in over a day. He did not want to make a detour to Altadena. They drove back to their daughter's apartment. Ashley slept on the couch, giving her parents the bed. Their house gone, their lives upended, Loyda looked at her daughter and at least felt safe. Rosie, their dog, was there, too.

It's going to be OK, Loyda thought.

As they laid their heads down to get some rest, Eric Mendoza of Sixty-Nines and Tim Larson of Twenty-Threes were still at work in the Palisades. James Stratton of Manhattan Beach Fire was, too. In Altadena, Gunner Alves and Captain Joshua Swaney of County Fire Twelves were still on the clock, as was Jake Torres with Nineteens. And so were thousands more across Los Angeles County, as containment was a long way off and fires continued to burn.

19

"The Parrots!"

LOYDA AND HERB (AND ROSIE) RETURNED TO ALTA-dena around six thirty on Thursday morning. They parked on Santa Anita Avenue, about a mile and a half away from McNally Avenue. California Highway Patrol and LA County Sheriff's deputies had formed checkpoints around the perimeter of the fire to keep curious residents like them away from the still-smoldering ruins of their neighborhoods, but they were able to slip through, walking through the hellscape toward their home as the sun rose.

As they came upon their street, they could see on the corner their neighbor's home still standing. A rush of happiness came over Herb, who was wearing jeans and a TaylorMade baseball cap—he was an avid golfer—along with an N95 mask. But after several steps more, he could see that the rest of the entire block had been wiped out.

"Oh my God."

There was nothing. Nothing.

This is not even real, Herb thought. Smoke was still rising from their home. None of their neighbors had made it back yet. So, he and Loyda started taking pictures of their home and of their neighbors'. The sun was massive as it rose, a pinkish-red through the hazy smoke blanketing the neighborhood. Loyda, in a black sweatshirt and an N95 mask, walked down her driveway, past their two burned-out cars with melted hubcaps, to see what, if anything, she could identify. Their Mercedes was unrecognizable.

How does fire do that?

Loyda, scouring their property—looking inside the cars, and for what she could get to of their home—spotted something.

"Look what I found!"

They were two small pins from UPS, where Herb and Loyda were working when they first met—commendations for his years of service. "Leadership. Spirit. America," one said. Herb took Rosie off her leash, and she immediately bolted into the backyard like she always would. When she returned, she came to the front yard and sat down, staring across the street. Herb immediately identified that she was sad. Grieving, even.

The Wilsons' block was more than a tight-knit group of neighbors—it was a reflection of Altadena as a whole. Nearly 20 percent of Altadena residents were African American. The city's diversity flourished in the 1960s and '70s, after discriminatory practices like redlining were outlawed, and Altadena became the center of a vibrant Black middle class. And while they had lived there for two decades, others on the block had spent lifetimes on McNally. Their neighbors were straight and gay, young and old, white and Black, Asian and Latino. Just like so many other streets in Altadena. Now so many of them were gone.

Herb held the UPS pins that Loyda had found.

"This is all that's left."

By Thursday morning, 17,234 acres had burned in the Palisades. When I returned there after spending the night in my own bed, the first sign of life I saw or heard other than firefighters, reporters, or residents who had snuck in was a wild bird.

The sound was unmistakable. On a hill atop the Palisades's Alphabet Streets, the neighborhood behind Sixty-Nines, I looked out over the hazy sunrise and heard the piercing squawk of a nanday parakeet.

Katy Tur was surveying with me, having flown in the night before to see the neighborhood of our youth incinerated. As she went off on her own, I looked out toward what I knew was the Pacific Ocean but could not see through the mix of marine layer and rising smoke.

Kree-ah! Kree-ah!

"The parrots!" I cried out—confusing the parakeets with their cousins on the other side of town. "Incredible."

The shrill call of the green wild birds caused me to look up and spot the distinct yellow chevron gliding down their backs. Seeing and hearing them filled me with an energy that had been sucked out of my body the last two days. They were alive. The Palisades was gone, but they had already come back. Unbeknownst to me, this family of birds had long been survivors of Los Angeles fires.

"In 1959, experts from the National Fire Protection Association surveyed portions of Los Angeles. They found a mountain range within the city. Combustible roofed houses closely spaced in brush-covered canyons and ridges serviced by narrow roads. They called it a 'design for disaster.'"

Those were the words of the actor William Conrad, narrator of a short 1962 documentary, produced by the LAFD, titled *Design for Disaster*, about the disastrous Bel Air Fire of 1961 in Los Angeles. That is when the yellow-headed amazon, with a rainbow gradient atop its head stretching forward to its beak, is reported to have found its way into the Los Angeles wild, as, according to the *Los Angeles Times*, "private aviaries were opened to save the birds. Many parrots escaped by chewing through their cages; all except heavy wrought-iron cages amount to about a day's work for a parrot's powerful beak."

Their cousin, the red-crowned parrot, is also easily spotted in and around parts of Los Angeles County that the Eaton Fire had devastated. Today there are more of them in Los Angeles than in their native range in Mexico, John McCormack of Occidental College's Moore Laboratory of Zoology, home to the Free-Flying Los Angeles Parrot Project, told me when I visited him after the fires to learn more about the birds that filled me with life when I needed it most.

The sound of the free-flying parrots is instantly recognizable to most Los Angeles County residents. Some find them incredibly annoying. A nuisance. Others marvel at the configurations they circle in until the birds—mostly green, but the variations of species also share shades of blue, yellow, red, and even purple—bed down in tree canopies from the Pacific Ocean to the San Gabriel Mountains.

Back in the Palisades, it was the nandays that had survived, and, less than forty-eight hours after the fires broke out in their adoptive home, they were back. Earlier in the morning, before the sun came up, I didn't know if I could make it through another day. I saw the sign advertising the real estate services of my sister-in-law, whose own family home was, we believed, gone, affixed to the chain-link fence of the destroyed Palisades Charter Elementary School. My parents had texted a watercolor of our former house, and the red bricks I saw crumbled to the ground the afternoon before looked so vibrant and beautiful in the painting, as did the white picket fence that had been charred grey. None of that would come back today. But the nandays did. And this morning, they were anything but annoying. They were finding their way back ahead of most humans. They gave me hope.

Exactly one year to the day before the National Weather Service issued the particularly dangerous situation warning, the Los Angeles City Fire Department posted *Design for Disaster* on its YouTube channel. The twenty-six-minute documentary on the Bel Air Fire was made as an after-action report and a warning about the dangers of living in what became known as the wildland-urban interface of Los Angeles. Nearly five hundred homes were destroyed, and sixteen thousand acres burned—numbers already surpassed between the devastation of the multiple fires still burning in Los Angeles after just two days.

That morning, before most people in reeling Los Angeles were awake, Donald Trump again took to his social media platform at 4:29 a.m. in Los Angeles:

> Fire is spreading rapidly for 3 days—ZERO CONTAINMENT. Nobody has ever seen such failed numbers before! Gross incompetence by Gavin Newscum and Karen Bass. . . . And Biden's FEMA has no money—all wasted on the Green New Scam! LA is a total wipeout!!!

In fact, FEMA's administrator was already on the ground in Los Angeles, arriving after President Biden promised 100 percent reimbursement—through the agency that Trump insisted "has no money"—for the first 180 days of fire recovery. Whether or not Trump understood it, the city and county had in some measure been through this before, and the circumstances were remarkably similar to another catastrophic fire that both then and now were due largely to the "climate," as the 1962 documentary emphasized, that makes Los Angeles so attractive to so many.

"Some move up to the scenic secluded hill areas, where lush California vegetation softens the ridges and valleys for miles in every direction, and breezes blow clean through native growth."

Those were the same conditions that fueled the Sunset Fire the night before. Now, thanks to heroic efforts of the mutual-aid response, and a break from the winds, it was largely extinguished. Evacuation orders for that fire, which grew to sixty acres, were lifted.

For about three hours, Loyda was searching for her wedding rings, which she had stopped taking on vacations because in the past she had misplaced them. She loved them so much, and now they were gone. Herb, sitting on the curb with Rosie, took in the stillness of their neighborhood. Like an ember, his pain was smoldering within, and fed by the elements around him, burning. He wondered how they ended up here, in this moment.

I'm not sure if it's a blessing or a curse that we missed having to evacuate. Sitting in the power outage. I bet it was almost hell on Earth.

From afar, they couldn't feel it until they got home. And when they did, the small things came back. Herb's autographed photograph of Malcolm X and Muhammad Ali that had hung in their living room. His golf clubs. The photograph from his grandson whose teeth were coming in framed next to a smiling photo of Herb. All they had were the carry-on bags they had brought with them to Hawaii.

After hours on McNally, the police began giving them a hard time about being there.

"What are you doing? You're not supposed to be here," they were told.

The couple began walking away from their house, not knowing when they'd be allowed back.

Katy Tur and I drove through the Palisades much like I had done the morning before, this time with a camera in the back seat. It was a surreal experience for two kids who grew up together in this neighborhood.

"If I was going home, I'd make a left on this street," she remarked as we approached Sixty-Nines on Sunset. We did.

We pulled up to a driveway where only a doorframe and the steps to it were still standing, with a potted succulent directly in front.

"Was that your front door?"

"Yeah, and this was the living room," she said. "We put a Christmas tree in this corner right here, and behind that was a bathroom where my dad set up a darkroom for me." A smile grew across her face. "I loved photography."

"Did you ever evacuate?" I asked her.

"No, we never evacuated."

"And that's what crazy. Everybody thought that in the event of a natural disaster, this area is untouchable," I said, referring to the Alphabet Streets, where Katy had lived at one point.

"They just thought fire would be contained before it got down here. Thankfully, it mostly was. Until now. And this is the most densely packed area in the Palisades."

"Not a single house is left here," I replied.

Katy stared off into the distance.

We made our way together to the Palisades Recreation Center, where the "new" gymnasium—built after our early childhood—had been destroyed. But the original one, made of brick and built in 1947—the first post–World War II civic building built in the Palisades, according to the Pacific Palisades Historical Society—still stood. Affixed to it was a plaque dated March 22, 1986, five days before my third birthday, that commemorated the installation of a new children's playground.

"DEDICATED TO THE KIDS . . . OUR NEW CHILDREN'S PLAYGROUND AREA."

Names of dozens of donors were immortalized in bronze. The first two at the top were my parents. "Patti & Steven Soboroff."

I took a photograph of the plaque at 8:24 a.m., just as I had at 3:21 p.m. on January 3, four days before the fire started, when I last visited the park with my wife, kids, middle sister Hannah, her husband, and their children—including their brand-new baby boy, their fourth. This park was my dad's pride and joy—and a pivotal moment in launching his nearly half-century career in public service.

"$45,000 Repair Campaign: Playground Partisan Swings Into Action," a *Los Angeles Times* headline read exactly thirty-nine years to the day I stood in front of the plaque in the destroyed park.

> "When people pack lunch boxes to go to Palisades Park with their kids, they take sandwiches and Band-Aids," said Steven L. Soboroff.
>
> Soboroff is so displeased with the run-down condition of play equipment at the 46-acre park in Pacific Palisades that he has single-handedly undertaken the task of raising $45,000 to refurbish the play area.
>
> Soboroff, a Palisades resident whose children are 2½ years and 7 months old, started his formal fund-raising about a month ago. He already has raised $23,000 in amounts ranging from $5 to $15,000. "I'm also working on a $10,000 anonymous pledge," he said.
>
> . . .
>
> Delores Averill, district supervisor for the Los Angeles Department of Recreation and Parks, said the city does not have the money to buy new playground equipment. She applauded Soboroff's efforts, calling him "one of the few genuine philanthropists."
>
> . . .
>
> "I handle investments representing department stores,"

> Soboroff said. "This is an investment with a different kind of return. Sometimes you smile when you make money. Sometimes you smile when you see kids playing at a park."

The playground equipment my parents had raised the money for was long gone, and what had replaced it had melted in the fire atop the sand. But the plaque commemorating it was still there. I sent the photo to my family group chat. Hannah replied with eight broken heart emojis, one for each of my parents' grandchildren, including the one who would be born in a few weeks.

20

"Open Up the Water Main"

"GOVERNOR GAVIN NEWSCUM SHOULD IMMEDIATELY go to Northern California and open up the water main, and let the water flow into his dry, starving, burning State, instead of having it go out into the Pacific Ocean," the president-elect sent out through his social media website at 11:36 a.m. Los Angeles time. "It ought to be done right now, NO MORE EXCUSES FROM THIS INCOMPETENT GOVERNOR. IT'S ALREADY FAR TOO LATE!"

The Washington Post reported that Trump's obsession with this "fish tale," as the newspaper called it, likely went back to a failed deal for a golf course that he wanted to develop in Fresno, in California's Central Valley, hundreds of miles from Los Angeles:

> According to the Congressional Research Service, farmers already get most of the water that is delivered via the federally run Central Valley Project—about 5 million acre-feet (1.629 trillion gallons) a year. An additional 600,000 acre-feet goes to municipalities and industry, 410,000 acre-feet to wildlife refuges and 800,000 acre-feet to fish and wildlife needs. That means farmers get more than 70 percent of the water in the Central Valley. Another

> network, the California-run State Water Project, delivers about 70 percent of its water to urban users, including 25 million people in the San Francisco Bay Area, Central Valley and Southern California.

There was not any water to send to Los Angeles from the Central Valley. But that didn't stop Donald Trump from fanning the flames of misinformation. Gavin Newsom, for his part, would insist he was stress-testing every theory thrown at him about the fires, even as containment was next to zero and as many of his own constituents believed he, at best, was not doing enough or, at worst, was to blame.

"Whose reservoir is that?" he wondered after first hearing about the City of Los Angeles's Santa Ynez Reservoir, above the Palisades, sitting dry for nearly a year while local officials struggled to execute a plan to repair tears in a protective cover meant to prevent contamination. Dozens of city fire apparatuses sitting in a repair yard near downtown Los Angeles also made headlines later.

"I want redundant systems. Give me the best practices across the globe. Bullshit the pressure goes off. I want to know. And why did it happen in Altadena and the Palisades?"

In the moment, Newsom was asking himself the same questions as so many others about how these Great Los Angeles Fires became so devastating. About whether any amount of firefighters or equipment or water could have stopped the conflagration fueled by the mountain wave phenomenon predicted by the National Weather Service days before. About why or why not a company was pre-positioned in a particular area. About how winds could have shifted for some homes at just the right time. Or how a hardened structure with defensible space was able to allow one to survive just long enough.

One of those structures was the temple my family belonged to in the Palisades. As Trump was shooting off messages into cyberspace, I was there, inside Kehillat Israel, with the cantor, Chayim Frenkel, who had presided over my Bar Mitzvah, while the temple was still under construction, in the Lutheran church next door. Both houses of worship were still standing. Also with us were the two rabbis, Amy Bernstein and Daniel Sher, who I didn't know personally. I had picked up the three of them to bring them back to see the temple and let us inside.

"Everything across the street from the synagogue burned down, but the synagogue is still here," I observed. "What's it like to see it?"

"Surreal," said Sher.

"Unbelievable," seconded Bernstein.

We walked in, with Bernstein pulling her spry German shepherd puppy along with us. The temple was heavily fortified, constructed from fire-resistant material in 1997, replacing the original building of the congregation, founded in 1950. The smell of smoke was pungent as we rounded the switchback staircase from the garage up to the atrium outside the sanctuary. On the ground was ash that had blown in under the doors to the terrace outside. Bernstein was sobbing.

"I can't believe it's still here. It's the only hope I have left," she wailed as she covered her eyes and face, wrapped in a half-hug by Sher. "I'm so glad it's here." Both rabbis had lost their homes to the fires.

"The remnants of the Palisades is right here," Frenkel said, pointing to the ashes.

I had not been back to this temple in many years. But returning, especially as we walked into the sanctuary, was overwhelming.

"This is the community in which I went to preschool," I said to them. "My siblings had their Bar and Bat Mitzvahs here."

"This is now a refuge for the entire community," Frenkel said, reminding me that a third of his congregation—the number of people that could fill the giant and brightly lit sanctuary we now stood in—had lost their homes. In front of the arc that held the congregation's Torah before it was removed during the evacuation, I asked him—knowing how soothing and beautiful I had found his voice over so many family milestones, including weddings and funerals—to sing.

"When disaster strikes, we turn to our faith. And that's what this represents," he began. "I sing this lovingly for our community to heal."

He and Bernstein, joined in harmony, sang the Shema, a prayer reaffirming that faith. Though I had moved away physically and spiritually from this place, in that moment, I felt I was exactly where I was supposed to be.

The cameras from atop Mount Wilson, at over 5,700 feet, had captured the earliest moments of the Eaton Fire on Tuesday night. The Mount Wilson Observatory housed what was the largest telescope in the world until the middle of the twentieth century, and it is still a popular destination for amateur and professional astronomers alike. The video feed coming from Mount Wilson, affixed to critical communication infrastructure for televisions, phones, and emergency responses, was no longer showing a fire in the distance but one at the feet of the towers from which the robotic cameras were panning. And as Katy Tur and I stood together live on her broadcast across the street from where Cathay Palisades once stood, I saw out of the corner of my eye the feed from Mount Wilson, placed side by side with us as we were talking.

Katy pointed out what we were seeing, and I, in real time, had a realization of how consequential the firefight on Mount Wilson would be.

"Those are repeaters, as you know," I said. "You know this as well as I do. The communication system, especially for law enforcement as well, works with a series of repeaters up on top of Mount Wilson.

"And so, think about being the emergency services that work in this county that rely on these towers that we're looking at right now," I continued as smoke climbed to the summit and swirled around the foot of them. "They're critical to law enforcement and first responder responses like the ones we've been seeing. So there is no more critical infrastructure in Los Angeles than what you're looking at on the left-hand side of your screen."

Almost on cue, a giant Super Scooper airplane that had been making rounds between the Palisades and the Pacific Ocean flew over—a sign that the arial attack was back in full force not only in the Palisades but also likely heading to the fire we were watching play out on the monitor to our left in the street. Larry Welk, the veteran news chopper pilot who'd watched the Eaton Fire explode from the landing pad at the Jet Propulsion Laboratory on Tuesday night, joined us on camera to describe the importance of the moment we now found ourselves watching play out.

"It's critical to get the arial assets," he said, reminding us that fires had burned up to the fire observation post and observatory previously. "They will most likely not lose any of the equipment. They've got very good brush clearance up there. And the winds, as you've pointed out, Katy, are cooperating today." Other Super Scoopers flew by, giving all of us a sense of relief, at least in the immediate term. But with two thousand structures now confirmed lost, five people reported dead, and at least five fires burning, we knew we were not out of the woods. In the Palisades, fire had burned over 17,200 acres; in Altadena, over 10,600; the Hurst was approaching 1,000 in the northern San Fernando Valley; Woodley at around 60 acres in the Sepulveda Basin; and now the Lidia Fire, at almost 350 in Acton, where Palisades firefighter

Eric Mendoza lives with his wife and two daughters, who had not heard from or seen him in days.

Mendoza had been driving around the Palisades—sometimes in the fire station's pickup truck to allow access to areas blocked by fallen debris—putting out whatever fires they could. Near Will Rogers Park, the backdrop to my Tuesday-night live reports, they found a home that had been abandoned. Smoke was coming from the attic.

"Hey, you guys see smoke?"

"Yeah, there's smoke."

In the pickup truck, they didn't have water in a tank, and the home's garden hose had no pressure, either. They did whatever they could, breaking parts of the house to get the embers off of it. With no water—and, assuming the house was a goner—they left. But when they returned to the house later, they discovered that another fire company—with an engine—had come and extinguished the flames, and saved the house. As they rolled through the Palisades—their first-in completely obliterated—it seemed impossible to believe there were still fires left to fight.

OK, this is it. No more. We're done with this.

The thought would quickly give way to a flare-up and then to a knockdown. All while Mendoza's chest felt like he had an elephant sitting on it from the many hours of smoke he had inhaled. It was a feeling that hundreds if not thousands of other firefighters were likely experiencing.

As Tim Larson of Twenty-Threes recalled, the place looked like it had gotten firebombed. Driving around the Highlands, where the fire started and where he remained for days, he felt like he was navigating through bombed-out ruins in "a World War II tank."

You don't see the steel twisted like that because we got ten companies putting water on it.

As they opened fire safes for residents, the insides were like ovens. Burnt papers. Guns melted. Larson was a young firefighter during the 1992 civil unrest in Los Angeles. It didn't even come close to this, he said. Larson's three sons—twenty-five, twenty-three, and seventeen—didn't initially believe the stories he told them about fire's immense power, until they saw the destruction for themselves.

Larson, like Mendoza, didn't live in the city, but he knew that the implications for his home neighborhood were chilling. His community, Newbury Park, about halfway between the Palisades and Oxnard, is also situated in foothills. And he couldn't help but think this could come for him, too.

If it came over here in the right wind, it could burn down my whole community.

What he was experiencing, what he had witnessed, and what was still playing out in front of his eyes was far beyond the worst-case scenario that he and the others at Twenty-Threes had ever imagined.

On Thursday afternoon, journalists entered the Roosevelt Room at the White House, where President Biden was holding a briefing about the Los Angeles Fires after having returned from the funeral of former president Jimmy Carter. Donald Trump had been in attendance, too. And the allegations he had been slinging about the causes of the fires had made their way onto the outgoing president's radar.

"It's not just about raking the leaves under the trees," Biden said, getting a dig at his predecessor and soon-to-be-successor's favorite line about forest management. Biden went on to defend the response of local officials in the face of Trump's relentless attacks. He emphasized that climate change, poor infrastructure, and combustible materials of everyday life weren't the only causes of the hurt in Los Angeles. Misinformation was as well.

"It'd be a lot easier if these—these electric lines are running underground," the president said, pivoting to ask Dave Turk, the deputy secretary of the Department of Energy, about the above-grade power lines that caused so much concern for firefighters like Chief Robert Garcia of the Angeles National Forest.

"In some places, it's absolutely necessary. And we need to have the funding and support to do that as quickly as we can," Turk replied.

"You do—all do a hell of a job," the president said to those assembled, including Vice President Kamala Harris, seated to his right, and, on his left, Liz Sherwood-Randall, assistant to the president as well as homeland security advisor and deputy national security advisor. Also in the room were General C. Q. Brown Jr., chairman of the Joint Chiefs of Staff, and Randy Moore, chief of the US Forest Service—Robert Garcia's boss.

Biden, whatever his mental state or acuity was in the final days of his presidency, stated clearly that this would be a defining moment for America's response to the fires of the future.

"The more we can explain to the American people in plain, straightforward, honest English, or whatever language they best understand, what exactly is happening, the more we're likely to get the kind of support and not make a political deal out of this. I'm leaving this office very shortly. But it's not about the politics. It's about giving people some sense of security that we're going to be able to get this under control. But it's going to take time."

The clock was ticking. And Donald Trump was not on the same page.

As the president wrapped up his remarks, a reporter asked, "Do you trust that California will get the aid they need in the next administration?"

"I'm not in a position to answer that question. I pray to God they will."

By late afternoon in Los Angeles on Thursday, January 9, a sixth fire had ignited in the West Hills area—the western portion of the San Fernando Valley, in an area where the Santa Ana winds had again started blowing from the northeast. Soon helicopters were visible, dropping water. And soon after that, hot shot crews—elite strike teams of firefighters dispatched from different jurisdictions and trained to deal with the most challenging wildfire scenarios—marched along the ridge line through the red phosphorus fire retardant that had been dropped before they arrived.

As those scenes played out, Katy Tur and I stood together high above the Palisades while the sun started to set behind us. As word of the new firefight reached us, the green fire engines of the US Forest Service rolled by—not anywhere near a national forest but on the streets of the Palisades.

"It feels like help is here," I told Joy Reid when we joined her on the air.

Joy asked me to debunk the "lies, misinformation, disinformation about who is to blame for the fire. About whether or not the fire services were allowed to use water."

"We've talked to people locally today who said the reason the water may not have been at the pressure they wanted it to be was just because of simple overuse," I explained. While I wasn't aware at the time of the Santa Ynez Reservoir's 117-million-gallon reserve being empty, I had heard that "the [three million-gallon] tanks were full to the maximum capacity," which they were. The larger point was that even if the Santa Ynez Reservoir had increased or sustained pressure, the Los Angeles Department of Water and Power maintained that its own system had enough water, and that the confluence of factors is what made the fire what it was.

What *was* simple to see was how the embers of misinformation were spreading farther and wider than any fire in Los Angeles. Far-right conspiracy theorist Alex Jones claimed he had "basic evidence that the Democratic Party with their policies are one hundred percent responsible—*consciously*—for the historic fire destroying much of Los Angeles in the last forty-eight hours."

Elon Musk responded to a post on his website of the clip from *The Alex Jones Show*—headlined "Los Angeles Fires Are Part of a Larger Globalist Plot to Wage Economic Warfare & Deindustrialize the Untied [sic] States Before Triggering Total Collapse" with one word:

"True."

He deleted it later, but not before Jones—who'd claimed that the 2012 shooting at Sandy Hook Elementary School was a hoax—himself gloated about it on his broadcast.

Chris Hayes responded on air to Jones: "The absolute barrage of garbage. Of filth. Of sewage being just pumped into the brains of people is unbelievable. It starts to feel kind of like a collective informational suicide we're all committing."

By ten o'clock on Thursday night, the Eaton Fire was approaching fourteen thousand acres, and the Palisades Fire was nearing twenty thousand. National Guard troops deployed by Governor Newsom five hours earlier began rolling to staff the fire perimeters of the evacuation zones, securing them so that the ongoing firefights and early recovery efforts could get underway.

"Helping everybody, that's what we're here for, what I signed up to do," said a guardsman in camo fatigues with the name *Vega* visible across his chest.

After nearly sixty-one hours on the air of continuous breaking news coverage, the anchors, producers, reporters, technicians, and other members of the KNBC team took their first break, signing off until they would resume broadcasting in the early morning, as the death toll rose to ten between the Palisades and Eaton Fires.

"A long road to recovery on this. It may be too early for people to even think about rebuilding, but I guarantee you—I've been here for a long time," veteran anchor Colleen Williams—who started on KNBC the same year my parents fixed up the park in the Palisades, 1986—said, "people in this town are resilient. They will rebuild."

21

"My Lungs Are Not Expanding"

"HEY, GO GET SOME REST. GO HOME," CAPTAIN BROWN TOLD FIRE-fighter Eric Mendoza Friday morning, the third day of the Palisades Fire, with other firefighters available to relieve the veteran.

Mendoza went right to his truck—where some kind of black stuff had melted in the interior, and the smell of smoke filled the cabin. He had been working around the clock since the moment that he and the rest of Sixty-Nines raced to the Palisades Highlands before the first call about the fires even came in. As hard as it was to leave his fellow firefighters at the station, he knew he was in trouble. *I need to get home*, he thought.

He got into his car and bolted for the freeway. He was flooring it. Mendoza's lungs hurt so badly, he continued to feel like he could barely breathe. Once he hit the 405 Freeway and got cell phone reception, he called his wife and daughters.

"I'm coming home."

After two and a half days of not being able to reach him, they were shocked.

"What?"

"I'm on my way home."

When he walked in the door, they were all in tears. They could not believe what they were seeing. But as soon as Mendoza crossed the threshold of his home, he collapsed.

"What's wrong?" his wife asked.

"I just—my lungs are not expanding," he told her, gasping. "I need to go to urgent care."

They rushed to get him a blood oxygen saturation test, and his levels were at around 89—a level deemed dangerously low. In need of oxygen and shots of corticosteroid, he got immediate treatment from a doctor and was placed on two weeks' leave, during which time he was to undergo a battery of tests. Though Mendoza was relieved to be home and so grateful to see his family, as the adrenaline wore off, all he could think about was his band of brothers.

I love this job. I love the department. I love being a fireman.

I first met Albino Fuentes when I was just a kid. He worked at Mort's Deli, the legendary Jewish delicatessen on Swarthmore, in the heart of the Palisades. I can still taste the matzoh ball soup and steak fries when I think about it. Albie, as we called him, worked behind the long stainless-steel counter where you placed your order before moving right to left with a red tray that would match the color of his hat and apron. When Mort's closed in 2007, Albino moved across Sunset and around the corner to work at Café Vida, where he became the heart and soul of the place. Every time we'd go in, he'd give us a hug and ask about whatever part of the family wasn't there.

When I told Nicolle Wallace on Wednesday afternoon that the Palisades's DNA was just as much made of the people who *don't* lay their heads here at night, I was thinking of Albino. And that's why I asked him to meet me to come see what had happened himself. I picked him up in Santa Monica, along with one of his daughters, and we drove to the remains of the Palisades Business Block. We parked the Wagoneer and walked down the street, my left arm around Albino's back, my hand resting on his left shoulder. He was wearing his black Café Vida T-shirt and black pants—the uniform we were so used to seeing him in.

"Oh my God. Oh my God," he said as we approached the remains of his workplace, his voice cracking.

"So many beautiful memories. All my kid friends. All my young friends. All my old friends." I asked him what he wanted them to know. "You know, I love you, and I'm going to miss you so much," he replied. "But we're going to bring this back. OK? We have to bring it back because it's too much love."

Albino told me about how on a recent work day at Café Vida he gave each of his two favorite customers—Ben and James—a hat from his native Oaxaca, Mexico, where he had just returned from visiting. "I remember I took a picture with them, not knowing it was going to be the last picture of me with my customers."

As he cried from behind his orange-tinted glasses, I pulled him in for a big hug, his head resting inside my right shoulder and mine on the back of his head. I needed it as much or more than he did.

"It's just so hard, *hijo*, to digest all this. But we're still on our feet. We're still on our feet, and we're going to come back."

"I think you represent," I told him, "what I think makes this community special. Which is the relationship that people who are from here have with people who come here to work. Who make this place go. And I just want you to know that I believe—and I'm sure so many people here believe—there's no Palisades without Albie."

He reached out, and we held hands.

"And without your colleagues here," I continued. "And everybody who makes this community go."

"I'm here," he said, "and I promise I'll be here."

"You better!" I told him.

After we left Café Vida, I drove Albie, my brother Miles, and my friend Jake Levine—who had joined me in the Palisades—to see Katy Tur during her broadcast. She was speaking live with chef and restaurateur José Andrés and actress Jennifer Garner, who were on the ground to deliver relief through World Central Kitchen and Save the Children, respectively. I joined them on the air, talking about having been with Albie moments before. Garner, who said she had eaten at Café Vida "a hundred million" times, agreed that he and others who worked in the service industry in the Palisades are "the staple of the community."

When we got off the air, I introduced Chef Andrés to Albino. As they stood face-to-face, their hands placed on each other's shoulders, I stood at a distance to watch a man who I had first met after we'd both returned from Ukraine—a man who has made it his life's mission to feed others in crisis, which drove him to found World Central Kitchen—connect with a man whose life's mission has been to feed so many in the Palisades. By the time we posted the report about Albino online, his daughter had set up an online fundraiser for him that raised nearly $60,000.

Standing there watching, Levine, back in the Palisades in his capacity as a displaced resident and not as a White House official, wondered what, if anything, he could do to help.

By midafternoon on Friday, January 10, 2025, Gavin Newsom had invited the president-elect to visit California to see the devastation for himself. In a single-page letter, the governor extended an olive branch to the man who had repeatedly called him Newscum over the past several days.

Dear Mr. President-elect,

It was just six years ago that we toured the devastation of the Camp Fire in the town of Paradise, the deadliest wildfire in California's history. That day, you also visited the Woolsey Fire near Malibu, which took the lives of three residents and displaced tens of thousands. Communities, traditions, places—wiped out in a matter of hours. You witnessed firsthand the heartbreak and destruction that all too many places across this nation have faced from more frequent and more severe natural disasters—fires, hurricanes, and floods.

Now California is again facing one of the most destructive fires in our history. On Tuesday, January 7, a massive windstorm hit Southern California, with hurricane-force gusts nearing 100 miles per hour in Los Angeles County. Southern California has seen virtually no rain this winter, and when those winds swept through the parched landscape, tiny ignitions became raging wildfires. Those fires, including the Palisades, Eaton, Hurst, Lidia, Woodley, and Kenneth Fires, have devastated the greater Los Angeles area, even in the face of Herculean work by legions of experienced firefighters. Tens of thousands of acres have burned. Thousands have lost their homes and businesses. At least ten people are reported to have died. The loss and devastation are horrific.

We are thankful that President Biden has swiftly approved our major disaster declaration—a strong indication of the partnership California needs and

> appreciates with any federal administration. However, the threat to lives and property remains acute. Higher-than-normal winds of up to 70 miles per hour are still forecast for the next several days, and more extreme winds are likely early next week, with no change to dry conditions.
>
> As you prepare to assume the presidency once more, I invite you to come to California again—to meet with the Americans affected by these fires, see the devastation firsthand, and join me and others in thanking the heroic firefighters and first responders who are putting their lives on the line. In the spirit of this great country, we must not politicize human tragedy or spread disinformation from the sidelines. Hundreds of thousands of Americans—displaced from their homes and fearful for the future—deserve to see all of us working in their best interests to ensure a fast recovery and rebuild.

Newsom signed the letter, "With respect and an open hand," while suspecting that something about their relationship—in which, even as adversaries, they'd been able to put politics aside in times of crisis—had changed. Now he waited for Trump to respond. That night, any thought that the Palisades Fire might have been waning vanished into the newly energized smoke, continuing to grow beyond twenty-one thousand acres—now threatening homes in Brentwood, to the east of the Palisades. The now-familiar glow from the darkness was trying to climb over the Santa Monica Mountains, too, toward the south side of the San Fernando Valley.

22

"Clip That Son of a Bitch"

I ARRIVED IN ALTADENA AROUND TWO O'CLOCK ON Saturday afternoon and drove straight to McNally Avenue. Herb and Loyda Wilson weren't there. Nor was Cate Heneghan. The place was a ghost town. But this is where Gavin Newsom wanted to meet and where Bianca Seward and our NBC News crew had set up shop for an exclusive interview that would air on the network's *Meet the Press* the following morning.

While I understood the numbers behind the fire, my first visit to the remains of the neighborhood was a shock I hadn't expected. It looked as bad as the Palisades—if not worse. Every house on the block and every block around it was gone. While we waited for the governor, who was at LAX greeting the arrival of a brigade of specialized Mexican firefighters, I left our crew to go see more of Altadena for myself.

I drove out to Fair Oaks, where Mike and Monique Bagby had fled their home in the earliest hours of Wednesday morning after determining that the block was no longer safe. I made a right and went up to Altadena and drove until I hit Side Pie, the pizza place where we'd held our son's ninth birthday in December. It was gone—nothing was left.

At that party, we had walked nearly his entire class from an indoor playground across Lake Avenue and down Altadena Drive, then through the back alley to the colorful tables in the courtyard to eat. I took a photo, then a video, and texted it to my wife, Nicole. The Pasadena Waldorf School in Altadena, where some friends of ours sent their children, was also destroyed. As I rolled by, I captured video of that, too.

When I returned to McNally, I waited in front of the home that we had picked to conduct the interview. Asymmetrical stone pavers cut through the singed grass that led to a triple-arched entryway, but above and beyond it there was nothing. No roof. Only the white, ashy debris, which had scattered with the winds. The giant oak trees of the block cast a shadow on the facade as the sun started making its way toward the horizon. When Governor Newsom pulled up, it was from the south part of the block, past the curb that Herb Wilson sat on two days earlier as he stared out at what once was.

Wearing a blue NBC News windbreaker, the first time I had reported in anything but my yellow fire jacket in days, I shook Newsom's hand, and we almost immediately jumped into the interview, for which I'd prepared with *Meet the Press* moderator Kristen Welker, executive producer David Gelles, and their entire team.

"Governor Gavin Newsom, welcome back to *Meet the Press*," I began.

"Good to be with you."

We started with the basics.

"Six different wildfires raging right now. Do you have the resources to combat all these fires at this hour?"

"Yeah, we have 14,000 people working the line right now. We doubled the National Guard. We have 1,680 out there helping on the logistics side. I was just with folks from Mexico, 73 folks will be relieving some of our hand crews. We've got nine states that are now providing under this EMAC [Emergency Management

Assistance Compact] system support. So we've got the resources. But more important—I've said this—we have the winds that have changed. And that allows us to be more resourceful with existing resources, particularly the aerial resources."

We spoke about the mission of the National Guard—to focus on additional fire prevention and to maintain order—and then I asked him about the magnitude of what was still unfolding.

"In your opinion, is this or will it be the worst natural disaster in the history of the United States?"

"I think it will be in terms of just the costs associated with it, in terms of the scale and scope. Don't even remind the folks in California, we had the Tubbs Fire, fifty-six hundred houses were lost. And, of course, Camp Fire, we had eighteen thousand housing units lost and eighty-five people that lost their lives. Currently we're getting confirmation from the coroners, so we always have to be careful on the death toll, but it's in the thirteen range, and I've got search and rescue teams out. We've got cadaver dogs out. And there's likely to be a lot more."

Thirteen was a higher number than I had heard before. I also knew Newsom wanted to make an announcement about suspending certain regulations, so I asked him what that entailed.

"I'm worried about time to getting these projects done," he told me. "And so we want to fast-track by eliminating any CEQA requirements. I've got Coastal Act changes that we're making. I want to make sure when someone rebuilds that they have their old property tax assessments and that they're not increased. So all of that's been done in the executive order we just announced."

The California Coastal Act of 1976 and CEQA, the California Environmental Quality Act, were both landmark laws designed to protect the environment from unregulated development. Suspending them, it occurred to me, would be met with opposition from environmentalists in the state.

"CEQA, Governor, and the Coastal Act are both environmental regulations," I pointed out. "And if you're going to be suspending those temporarily, are you concerned about problems that may result from the suspension of those environmental regulations and the potential abuse by developers?"

He said he was and that his executive order accounted for potential abuse.

"You've also called for an independent investigation into the issues around water supply that we've seen. What are the questions that you're hoping to answer?"

"The same ones you're asking. Same ones that people out on the streets are asking, yelling about: 'What the hell happened? What happened to the water system?' And, by the way, was it just overwhelmed? That you had so much that was used? We drew it down?"

"President-elect Trump has blamed you for this crisis," I soon asked, having noticed their back-and-forth myself, even from within the fire zone. "He called you incompetent. What's your response?"

"Well, I called for him to come out, take a look for himself. We want to do it in the spirit of an open hand, not a closed fist. He's the president-elect. I respect the office. We have a president of the United States that within thirty-six hours provided a major disaster declaration." He went on to detail his close relationship with President Biden and to push back on the theories floated by Trump.

"The reservoirs are completely full, the state reservoirs here in Southern California. That mis- and disinformation I don't think advantages or aids any of us. Responding to Donald Trump's insults, we would spend another month. I'm very familiar with them. Every elected official that he disagrees with is very familiar with them."

"We do know though from reporting here locally that one reservoir that serves the Palisades was not full," I interjected about the Santa Ynez Reservoir.

"And that's exactly what triggered my desire to get the investigation to understand what was happening with that local reservoir," Newsom retorted. "That was not a state system reservoir, which the president-elect was referring to as it relates to the Delta and somehow connecting the Delta smelt to this fire, which is inexcusable because it's inaccurate. Also incomprehensible to anyone that understands water policy in the state."

"My understanding is that you have put a call in to President-elect Trump. Has he called you back?"

"No, that was months ago. That was after his victory. So I look forward to him again coming out here in the spirit of cooperation—"

"Well, forgive me for interrupting you, but you did invite him to come out here. Have you had any response?"

"No. No."

"Nothing."

"No."

Not only had Trump not returned his call following his 2024 victory, but Newsom never heard back from Trump after a call from the governor in the wake of his 2020 defeat by Joe Biden. The governor and I went on to talk about Californians who had been thrown off their homeowners insurance policies ahead of the fires.

"I mean, this is an issue—and, by the way, persists in California because of the acuity of the new realities. Hot's getting hotter. Dry's getting drier. Wet's getting wetter. These atmospheric rivers, all the flooding that we've experienced in California but also across the rest of the United States. You're seeing insurance rates through the roof," he said, not presenting a solution but rather an understanding of the severity of the problem.

Toward the end of the interview, I turned to the future.

"Over the course of the next several years, Los Angeles will be host to the World Cup, and then the Super Bowl, and then the Olympics. With this rebuilding effort needing to take place, is LA going to be ready for all those global events?"

After going out of his way to compliment President-elect Trump for his work securing the Olympics, Newsom looked ahead.

"We're already organizing a Marshall Plan. We already have a team looking at and reimagining LA 2.0, and we are making sure everyone's included, not just the folks on the coast, people here that were ravaged by this disaster."

"You just said you're organizing a Marshall Plan for the rebuilding of California. What is that Marshall Plan?"

"For this region. We're just starting to lay it out. I mean, we're still fighting these fires, so we're already talking to city leaders. We're already talking to civic leaders. We're already talking to business leaders, with nonprofits. We're talking to labor leaders," he explained. "We're starting to organize how we can put together a collection of individuals on philanthropy for recovery, how we can organize the region, how we can make sure that we are seeking federal assistance for the Olympics more broadly, but also federal assistance for the recovery efforts and how we can galvanize the community with folks that love this community to really develop a mindset so that, at scale, we're dealing with the scope of this tragedy and responding to it at scale with efficiency—like the executive order I talked about—time value of delivering projects, addressing building codes, addressing permitting issues, and moving forward to rebuilding and being more resilient."

The voice in my earpiece—Gelles, the show's executive producer back in Washington—told me it was time to wrap it up, since we were filming what's known as live to tape—trying to stick as close as possible to the time we had allowed so we didn't have to trim much for time.

"Governor Gavin Newsom, thank you so much for joining us on *Meet the Press*."

"It's good to be back."

With that, Newsom and I took off our microphones and walked across the street to shoot what's known as B-roll—some images of us touring the neighborhood. When the mics were off, Newsom told me he was worried about the impact of the fire on the undocumented community, which he and I both knew would be central to the rebuilding effort. He told me he was going to meet National Guard troops who were stationed at the Eaton Fire perimeter and invited me to come with him. I hopped into the Wagoneer and followed his motorcade to the intersection of Fair Oaks and Woodbury, a half mile from where Cate Heneghan's neighbor contacted her at six o'clock on Wednesday morning. She had thought Fairoaks Burger was gone—but it still stood. Everything around it, however, was destroyed.

At the corner, two troops were standing guard to prevent residents and intruders from entering the neighborhood. One, last name Bocage, stood in his fatigues and with a face covering to keep out what we all believed was toxic air, his glasses peering out from between his soft cap and gator. Newsom stood with his hands in the back pockets of his jeans, just as he did on Tuesday as the fires broke out in the hills above the Pacific Coast Highway. The other guardsman talked intently with Newsom as I looked on next to their armored Humvee. Passersby had dropped off bottles of water and other provisions for them for what was the beginning of a mission without an expiration date.

* * *

I left Newsom—who had switched from his hotel in Beverly Hills to the InterContinental downtown to be proximate to both fires—and, for the first time in nearly a week, went to dinner with friends at Heavy Handed, a burger spot in the San Fernando Valley. The drive there—westbound on the 210 Freeway—was gorgeous, graced by a red-and-orange sunset like the one the night before the fire, this one made even more vibrant by the filthy air hovering over Los Angeles. My wife and kids were with my parents at their house in the Coachella Valley, and I was lonely. It was incredible to get to spend the time drinking a few beers and catching up with some of the crew—Ricky, Zoe, and Paul—we spend every New Year's Eve with camping in Santa Barbara County. Our last trip was the one when we sat around the campfire, and I had declared my aversion to covering wildfires.

After dinner, I made it home and went to bed early, long before President Trump sent another late-night online message.

> The fires are still raging in LA. The incompetent pols have no idea how to put them out. Thousands of magnificent houses are gone, and many more will soon be lost. There is death all over the place. This is one of the worst catastrophes in the history of our Country. They just can't put out the fires. What's wrong with them?

I woke up the next morning to appear live on *Meet the Press* from the Palisades to present my interview with Newsom. For his part, the governor's day started back in the Palisades, then revisited Altadena, and ended up back at the Palisades Fire, where the Mandeville Canyon neighborhood was now being threatened by flames.

When he returned Sunday night to his hotel, Newsom sat in his makeshift operations center, and Elon Musk was on one of the screens.

"What the hell is this?"

Musk was live-streaming a private briefing he was receiving from members of the Los Angeles County Fire Department after he had dropped off Tesla Cybertrucks and Starlink satellite dishes to be used for the relief effort.

"Are we doing private briefings now? What the hell is going on?"

Newsom laid into his team.

"I want to know exactly who—Jesus, guys, no one is allowed down there. So did he get escorted down there? Are we taking people off the front lines?"

Newsom, exhausted after traversing the city all day, was incensed.

"Now we're doing a private damn briefing, back down the other side of town where things are actually calmed down, and we're not abiding by this ridge fire?"

Newsom was talking over Musk—not really paying attention to the substance of the vertical live stream because he was so heated by the X chief's presence.

"By definition, I've allowed Elon Musk to come in! So, I just want to know what the hell is going on."

All of a sudden Musk, who had been taking up the firefighters' time for over ten minutes and was probing them about whether certain types of plants prevented brush clearance through regulation, looked as though he was about to wrap up, turning the camera around selfie-style.

"All right, sounds good!"

But instead of turning off the stream, Musk couldn't resist asking the firefighters a question about the theories pushed by Trump regarding water pressure. Newsom stopped cold and told everyone to listen.

"All right. What about water availability? Was water availability—I understand that was not an issue in Malibu, is that correct?" Musk asked.

"Water?" asked Los Angeles County Fire Battalion Chief Christian Litz, wearing his blue uniform, badge pinned to the left side of his chest above a pen tucked into his pocket, and blue baseball cap.

"Yeah," Musk replied.

"So, there was water, we have several reservoirs," as he pointed to them on a map. "Now, just an example, if we have one building burning, we can flow a thousand gallons a minute on that one building with the hose lays that we put in to stop it. You can imagine a thousand gallons per house we can do. The amount of water we're flowing, there really is no water system that's gonna keep that pace, so we have to bring in water tenders, which are these big tank water tanks—you know, twenty-five-hundred-, three-thousand-gallon trucks, and they'll come in, and that's what we have to do to compensate." He continued, referring to the Los Angeles Department of Water and Power, "DWP did a great job. They brought in big water trucks for us, and we used them as, basically, mobile hydrants."

"All right?" Musk replied sheepishly.

"All right," repeated the firefighter. "And then we have our own agency as well that has water tenders."

"Okay," Musk said. "My understanding is that along the—maybe the—correct me if I'm wrong—in Malibu along the coast there was no shortage of water; in the Palisades there was a shortage of water at a certain point, or is that not accurate?"

"Well," replied Litz, "we were flowing just an amount of water that the system couldn't—it was overbearing just because of how much water these firefighters were utilizing."

"Okay. All right. Sounds good," Musk said, seeming to recognize that a fight with the firefighters was likely not in his best interests.

"All right, thanks guys," he said to the live viewers, once again turning the camera back to selfie-style and abruptly cutting off his stream.

Newsom, watching slack-jawed with his team, barked an order to his communications director, Izzy Gardon.

"Izzy, clip that son of a bitch," the governor said. "I want that up there right now. This is goddamn proof! This is all bullshit and lies!" the governor said. "I'm done. Let's go on offense. Fuck these guys." The incoming fire he had been receiving from people, including close personal friends, that had been influenced by what was being spread online was too much. He had started blocking numbers of acquaintances. In fact, friendships with some of his oldest and closest allies ended because of it.

By 8:34 p.m., Musk's video was reposted on Newsom's X account.

"@ElonMusk exposed by firefighters for his own lies," the message read.

And with that, a new front had been opened in the extended attack on the fires, a battle to fight the "hurricane-force winds of mis-and-disinformation."

23

"If You Have, I Have"

I RETURNED TO ALTADENA TUESDAY MORNING, A FULL week since the crisis erupted. By then, the Eaton Fire had grown to over fourteen thousand acres, and the Palisades Fire, nearly twenty-four thousand. By then, at least twenty-four people—sixteen in Altadena (most in areas where evacuation warnings had not reached in time) and eight in the path of the Palisades Fire—had died.

When I arrived, the sky was blue, but little was left of Side Pie, the pizza place owned by Kevin Hockin and his wife, Rosanna Kvernmo. I had driven by it before interviewing Governor Newsom, but on January 14 I got out at the corner of Altadena Drive and Lake Avenue, around a mile from McNally Avenue, to meet up with the owners.

The restaurant's massive oven was covered in tiny tiles—yellow on the bottom, green in the middle, and they were still there. The top portion once had a mosaic of Stealie, the Grateful Dead's iconic skull logo, surrounded by more tiny tiles. Under the bricks that had fallen into the street and collapsed inside the structure, not much was recognizable—but I could see the beer fridge that held what I remember being every specialty brew I had ever seen. The bottles had exploded, the fridge had melted, and everything was tangled together.

Kevin and Rosanna's home survived. Their business did not. We had returned to see them for a story I wanted to do for *NBC Nightly News* about small businesses destroyed in the fire.

"I have thirteen, fourteen employees," Kevin told me. "And my heart breaks."

Their daughter's school, for now, was closed, too. We went around to the back courtyard where we'd had our son's birthday party, and to my surprise, all of the vibrant-colored tables—the kind you'd eat a school lunch at—were still there. They hadn't burned.

"When I saw the tables, I was like—oh, yes!" Rosanna explained in a way that made me smile. "This is definitely coming back!"

I couldn't fathom how she was thinking about that. Everything as far as you could see down Lake Avenue and up Altadena was destroyed.

"This community is so special, and it's really special to have a business here," she said.

I drove down Lake Avenue, past Rhythms of the Village, a store and community hub for music, art, and merchandise that centers around and honors the Chukwurah family's African heritage. Baba Onochie Chukwurah, the patriarch, is a musician who first came to the United States with the Nigerian musician Fela Kuti in 1969 and raised his family in Altadena. A professor of African language and history at California State University, Los Angeles, he is the heart of their family's store, run by his son, Emeka. I met them both as they held a drive to bring in supplies for people in the community at their home, which survived, not far from their store, which did not.

"I saw the shop fully ablaze," Baba Onochie told me, his hands expanding outward to illustrate the severity of the fire. "And I screamed. I felt sad. I felt all the emotions. And then I came to the conclusion that we can rebuild. And those are material things. What matters is that we're all alive."

Listening to him, and looking into his eyes, it was so easy to understand how the community they created together—centered around music, storytelling, and family—was a special one. A guy walked in to donate a large box of goods—bedding, clothes, and shoes, he said—and Emeka thanked him and led him to the back toward the garage to drop it off.

"That's the way I was raised," Baba Onochie told me. "Being communal. So it's almost divine that we're back here. Back at square one. And in a position to support anybody in need right now."

I couldn't believe their outlook.

"Even as you guys are hurting?" I asked.

"Yes, yes, of course," he and his son said in unison.

"That's our spirit," Emeka said.

"Because in my culture"—Baba Onochie told me about his Nigerian roots—"if you have, I have. If I have, you have."

I thanked them, and left, crossing paths with more members of the community who were dropping in to share with those who had nothing left.

The next day, I visited another charity drive in Altadena, this one hosted at the Pasadena Community Job Center, an affiliate of the National Day Laborer Organizing Network. I had met Pablo Alvarado, NDLON's co-executive director, during COVID, reporting on how day laborers and undocumented workers were often the "second responders" in moments of crisis—showing up to help others when society was often unable to help them.

The minute I pulled up, it was like that moment was repeating itself. Everywhere I looked, there were volunteers who had set up a drive-through drop-off, collecting items that the day laborers would distribute to members of the community in need. Then they would head out to do manual labor and physical cleanup of debris that still had not been removed, for fear that a stray spark or ember might reignite the flames. Pablo told me that thousands of people had come out over the course of the last week, and he showed me around, introducing me to people who would normally be home in the middle of a weekday or at work. He also explained that pitching in after a tragedy was nothing new for day laborers and undocumented workers.

"We've done it from Katrina, to Sandy, to Andrew. Everywhere in this country, day laborers have always been there to lend a hand."

We all went together on a cleanup effort where local residents joined day laborers to gather snapped branches, leaves, and anything else cluttering the streets of Pasadena—just outside of the evacuation zone—and load them into the backs of massive pickup trucks. Actress Eva Longoria was there too, after pledging $50,000 herself to the effort.

"Once the fires are put out, this is the community that's going to rebuild Los Angeles," she told me. She was right. And it was that exact community that Gavin Newsom told me off camera he feared would suffer most when President Trump was sworn in.

On Thursday, January 16, Chief Anthony Marrone of the Los Angeles County Fire Department walked into the Sinai Temple on Wilshire Boulevard for a meeting of Pacific Palisades community members who'd been displaced from their neighborhood. He made his way to the podium and apologized to deaf and hearing-impaired people in the audience.

"I didn't write any formal remarks, so I thought I would speak from the heart," said the thirty-nine-year veteran of the county fire department, who before that had begun his career in Beverly Hills and then became an LAFD medic.

Chief Marrone went through details of the response to the fires and what he called "the vital information you need." He also apologized, "not because we did something wrong, but because we were not able to protect a life, prevent a death, save your home, or save your business." After his remarks, he sat down. But a half hour later, the chief, who lives in the San Fernando Valley of Los Angeles—within city limits—felt compelled to return to the podium to answer a question he had heard from the audience.

"How do we prevent this from happening again?"

Marrone stalked up the steps to the dais and raised his hand to say he wanted to address the question himself.

"How do we prevent this from happening again?" he repeated. "That's going to be very, very difficult. Because we've had a lot of discussion, and we've had a lot of review, about the number of fire engines. The number of firefighters. How long did it take to get on scene? Did you have water? Or didn't you have water?"

Some of those questions had been raised already by Los Angeles City Fire Chief Kristin Crowley, when she spoke out to say that her department was under-resourced due to budget constraints. Investigative reporters were digging into allegations of dozens of idle fire trucks sitting in the city's maintenance yard near downtown or the controversy over the empty Santa Ynez Reservoir. But those were not the causes of the fire, nor of its severity, Marrone said.

"What we experienced here was a community conflagration much like Lahaina; the Marshall Fire in Colorado, when there was snow on the ground and fire moved from house to house; or Paradise in Northern California. What was different this time is that a community conflagration occurred in a metropolitan area . . . over two hundred fire stations. We have nine thousand firefighters in the Los Angeles County area between the twenty-nine departments."

He offered a prescription for the future.

"The challenge now is to build fire-wise communities. It's to make sure that when we rebuild, which will occur, that those structures are stand-alone. That a firefighter or fire engine is not going to be at your home for it to survive. We need to make sure that the defensive space is appropriate and that it's enough. And lastly, due to climate change, we need to manage our wildfire ecosystem. What we've essentially done in Los Angeles County is remove fire from the natural environment.

"When the Native First Peoples were here, the fires burned in these hills. And they even had cultural burns. We now no longer allow fire to propagate naturally, so when it occurs under hundred-mile-an-hour winds or seventy-mile-an-hour winds, it is impossible for Chief Crowley's firefighters, or my firefighters, to put that fire out. And this event was different. I've never seen fire behavior like that in thirty-nine years.

"This incident is going to go down as the most destructive fire incident in the history of Los Angeles County. We would love to be able to stop it next time. But I don't want to lie to you: it's going to be very difficult unless we change a couple of important things. So thank you for understanding that."

The audience applauded politely, and Marrone thanked them. Then he returned to his seat in the front row, unsure of when the Great Los Angeles Fires of 2025 would be contained or when the next one would come.

Epilogue

"Mop Up"

THREE DAYS AFTER THE IGNITION OF THE PALISADES and Eaton Fires, NOAA's National Centers for Environmental Information published its 2024 billion-dollar disaster analysis. The report is exactly what it sounds like. A list of "weather and climate disasters" with damage totaling one billion dollars or more. As the Great Los Angeles Fires continued to burn, undoubtedly climbing its way up the list, the federal agency said there had been "27 individual weather and climate disasters with at least $1 billion in damages, trailing only the record-setting 28 events analyzed in 2023."

The 2024 list was made up of two winter storm events, a wildfire event, a drought and heat wave event, a flooding event, six tornado outbreaks, five tropical cyclones, and eleven severe weather and hail events, NOAA said. They stretched across "many parts of the country." Since 1980, 403 events, adjusted for inflation, met that definition. But the frequency and intensity with which they have occurred are increasing, Adam Smith, the lead scientist for the project, wrote. And the likely cause was no mystery.

> Population growth and how and where we build play a big role in the increasing number and costs of billion-dollar

> disasters. But we also know from extreme event attribution research that human-caused climate change is increasing the frequency and intensity of certain types of extreme weather that lead to billion-dollar disasters—most notably the rise in vulnerability to drought, lengthening wildfire seasons in the Western states, and the potential for extremely heavy rainfall becoming more common in the Eastern states. Sea level rise is worsening hurricane storm surge flooding . . . Given those trends, it's likely that human-caused climate change is having some level of influence on the rising costs of billion-dollar disasters.
>
> Some mix of these factors is likely the reason that the 2010s decade was far costlier in the Billion-Dollar Disaster data set than the 2000s, 1990s, or 1980s, even when adjusted for inflation to current dollars.

During my ten years as a national broadcast journalist, many of the most costly events in America's New Age of Disaster took place. The Camp Fire in 2018, California's deadliest; Hurricane Maria in 2017, killing approximately 3,000 in Puerto Rico; Hurricane Harvey in 2017, dumping feet of rain and requiring nearly 20,000 rescues; severe heat and icing events that killed hundreds in the Pacific Northwest and Texas, respectively, in 2021; and the Hawaii firestorm in 2023 that was only survivable, for some, by jumping into the ocean.

I did not cover any of those disasters personally, but in the same period I've reported from my own share. That includes hurricanes Matthew and Irma in 2016 and 2017, respectively, in Florida. Also in 2017, I covered the deadly Thomas Fire in Ventura County, California. Yet despite the obvious and wide-scale devastation, whether the Great Los Angeles Fires will go down as one of the costliest weather or climate events ever in the eyes of the United States government remains uncertain.

That's because of efforts by the second Trump administration to refute, dismantle, or outright eliminate valuable resources within the federal government's arsenal to communicate about, respond to, mitigate, and prevent disasters.

Adam Smith today is the *former* lead scientist for the Billion-Dollar Weather and Climate Disasters program for NOAA. After the incoming Trump administration began implementing what it called "evolving priorities and staffing changes," in early March of 2025, Smith was informed verbally, he told me, to stop updating a database that tracked the financial toll of those hundreds of natural disasters dating back over forty years.

Today, at the top of the project's website, it reads "In alignment with evolving priorities, statutory mandates, and staffing changes, NOAA's National Centers for Environmental Information (NCEI) will no longer be updating the Billion Dollar Weather and Climate Disasters product."

Smith's conservative estimate of the financial toll from the fires was $50 billion. Now the federal government may never officially publish its estimation of the cost of the fires, a crucial measure that informs the insurance marketplace and would-be homeowners.

"We have to be more prepared now than ever," Smith told me after resigning his position in May 2025, which I reported with my NBC News colleague Nidhi Sharma. "And part of that is having data and information and a better understanding of what's possible. Unfortunately, with products like this one and many others being discontinued . . . it creates a kind of a vacuum in knowledge."

I was not aware of Smith's work stopping at the time. But it was around when he was waved off of working on the federal government's official tally of the cost of the Great Los Angeles Fires, and stopped keeping the list of America's costliest disasters entirely, that I finally started to understand how America's New Age of Disaster was not about climate change or cost alone. It was about that "vacuum of knowledge" Smith would later describe to me. And how, as I would come to understand, Smith himself was a prime example of why.

I was in Washington, DC, thousands of miles away from Los Angeles. In town to cover President Trump's Joint Address to Congress, I was running late for a clandestine dinner meeting set over the private messaging app Signal.

I had been working the phones all day from the NBC News Bureau on Capitol Hill, putting to use the sweet-talking skills I had honed during college working for Mayor Michael Bloomberg in New York City. Back then, I would call people to tell them why the mayor couldn't be at their Bar Mitzvah—"But he says mazel tov!"—or some other personal gathering. I graduated from intern to advance man, the most important job in politics you've likely never heard of. As a journalist, the skills I picked up as an eighteen-year-old NYU freshman have served me well, and on this day I was using them to convince federal workers fired by Elon Musk's Department of Government Efficiency to appear with me on MSNBC for a live on-air conversation before and after Trump's speech.

I had lined up young civil servants terminated from the Internal Revenue Service, the Department of Housing and Urban Development, the US Digital Service, and the US Forest Service to bravely speak about the real-world implications of losing the alphabet soup of federal employees and what this meant for our nation. I couldn't wait to sit down with them. But it was a near-retiree from the US Department of Health and Human Services (HHS) I was looking forward to seeing the most, at a Tex-Mex restaurant a few blocks from our bureau.

I was meeting Captain Jonathan White of the US Public Health Service Commissioned Corps. This wasn't our first get-together in this under-the-radar way. White was a central figure and important source for my 2020 book *Separated: Inside an American Tragedy*, about the Trump administration's family separation crisis.

White had been responsible for the mission to reunite the thousands of parents and kids ripped apart by Trump. Earlier, he had protested the separation policy from his post as a licensed and certified social worker running the Office of Refugee Resettlement (ORR) as its deputy director. White went on to star in *Separated*, the documentary that Oscar-winning filmmaker Errol Morris directed based on my book and released in theaters before the 2024 election.

In March 2025 he was still a government employee, and one with important thoughts to share about what I had witnessed firsthand in Los Angeles that January. The reason the principled insider who was trained as a social worker specialized in the needs of children at risk was the perfect person to talk to about the fires was because White had made a career shift within Health and Human Services.

When we last met like this in 2019—my notebook and pen in hand for hours at a Starbucks outside the city proper—Captain White had already left his job as the deputy director of the Office of Refugee Resettlement (ORR) and taken a senior role within the disaster recovery operation of HHS due to disagreements with his boss at the time, a Trump political appointee.

By the time we met up in 2025, in his current role as director of the Division of Community Mitigation and Recovery within HHS's Administration for Strategic Preparedness and Response,

White had "managed or deployed to in the field," as his LinkedIn profile highlighted, "more than 70 domestic disasters, public health emergencies, and humanitarian crisis events." That included when he led the reunification of all those separated children.

Family separation was an avoidable and man-made disaster. The Great Los Angeles Fires were not. At least they seemed that way, at first. But White wanted me to think differently, and reminded me that he had been to the aftermath of every federally declared mass-casualty fire in the last five years—including Los Angeles.

"Give me your notebook," White demanded as he—at warp speed—ran through some of the horrors he had seen in his current job, including the aftermath of the Lahaina fire on Maui, where survivors literally swam for their lives, and a clinic in Altadena that had literally burned through sideways.

I slid across the table my pen and the yellow-covered seven-by-five-inch spiral notebook I had grabbed on my way to cover Trump's inauguration from the border in San Diego six weeks prior.

"There will always be a fixation on proximate causes" in Los Angeles, White told me, "like hydrants running dry or a lack of available fire trucks. But that's a side story—not the main show. That avoids dealing with the *real* issue."

White drew an *X* across about two-thirds of the page and started scribbling furiously. Along the four arms of the X there were themes, all intersecting to create the Great Los Angeles Fires I had been a part of and was clamoring to understand better. They were:

- Global climate emergency
- Infrastructure disintegration
- Changes in how we live
- Politics of blame and disinformation

The climate emergency I witnessed in Los Angeles was part of a "large, ongoing global disaster," White said. "The hurricane in Asheville. Floods in the desert. We are objectively less safe than a few years ago, and we will be even less safe in ten years."

Fires, he said, have probably been the threat that has grown the most in those years. "And for many people depending on where they live, it will probably become the foremost," he later added. Fire "is a fast-growing part of the total threat matrix—everything is getting riskier but the increase in the threat level from fires is, for many people, the one that they will see the sharpest increase in in this decade."

Our infrastructure was obviously falling apart. "There's forty years of mitigation we haven't done," he maintained, echoing what many had pointed to already in the immediate aftermath of the fires. "We shouldn't have aboveground utilities!"

That disintegration's interaction with our modern way of living made the fire worse, he said.

"How?" I wondered.

"There were a thousand lithium ion batteries" that exploded and contributed to the fires.

"Yes! I saw and felt some of those explosions myself," I told him.

"Just like the propane tanks that fueled the Lahaina fire," White told me, to which he also responded after 102 people lost their lives.

Finally, the last arm of the *X* was the tone and tenor of our politics today. The result? Disinformation making disasters worse.

"Democrats are wrong that what we're facing is a future threat. And Republicans are wrong in saying there isn't one. The threat is here," White said as he prosecuted the case, breaking only briefly to enjoy his chips and guacamole.

What I had experienced, he told me, wasn't just a conflagration, like the Big Burn of 1910. It was "the fire of the future."

My eyes widened.

"The fire of the future," I repeated.

"Yes, the fire of the future."

"Changes are needed now." What had occurred in Los Angeles, he insisted, was "a sentinel event. It's a giant but addressable challenge."

This book won't solve the challenge that Captain White laid out before me. I'm not a civil engineer, or a climate scientist, or an urban planner, or someone with the ability to reverse the polarization in our politics. But I am a journalist guided by a simple principle: Report the facts on the ground as I always have done. To tell to you, as I always endeavor to do, what I saw, who I met, and what I learned during and after the Great Los Angeles Fires about America's New Age of Disaster.

Before we went our separate ways, Captain White going back to his work in disaster mitigation and recovery, I to reporting on the Trump administration's dismantling of the federal workforce, he left me with a parting thought.

What's needed, White said, especially with the gulf in income and opportunity between the affluent community of the Palisades and the middle-income neighborhood of Altadena, is empathy for those who experienced this tragedy. And not just empathy, but also empowerment of the community to influence decisions that will impact the recovery.

Recovery is a word many Angelenos still cannot fully wrap their heads around.

In July 2025, as I wrote this book, the death toll from the Eaton Fire rose from eighteen to nineteen, six full months after the fires' ignition. The remains discovered were believed to be of a seventy-four-year-old man who went missing the night of the fire half a mile from McNally Avenue, from where Cate Heneghan, the JPL senior engineer, and her neighbors fled.

In total, thirty-one people are confirmed to have died between the Eaton Fire and the Palisades Fire. Thousands of homes were destroyed. Almost forty thousand acres, nearly three times the size of Manhattan, burned in the most populous county, Los Angeles, in America.

In late March 2025, the *Los Angeles Times* reported that the "California Department of Forestry and Fire Protection released updated fire-hazard severity-zone maps for Los Angeles County for the first time in over a decade, adding more than 440,000 acres to the county's hazard zones, including a 30% increase in acres zoned in the highest severity rating." An ominous warning about the next fire as victims continued to reel.

As of this writing, in the early fall of 2025, the State of California says that despite over eighty thousand visits to disaster recovery centers in which nearly thirty-five thousand people received services and the distribution of almost $150 million in funds, not to mention an aggressive cleanup program that has removed most household waste and debris, just over 1,000 building permits had been issued as residents weigh how to rebuild or whether they can afford to. The "Marshall Plan" that Governor Newsom promised when we talked on McNally Avenue seems to many a long way off from his vision of "reimagining LA 2.0."

In the Palisades, my brother and sister-in-law, who lost everything when her parents' home, where they had been living, was destroyed, had their baby girl weeks after the fire. Their own home, which was under construction, survived despite all of their neighbors losing theirs, but like so many, they now are caught in a home insurance nightmare and unsure when, or if, they'll ever return.

James Kahn, the young man I met trying to save his parents' home, survived, as did their house, but the neighborhood did not.

Albino Fuentes found work outside of the Palisades, but remains forever tied to the community and its people.

Side Pie, the Altadena pizza spot, and Rhythms of the Village, the Chukwurah family's store and community hub, have not yet reopened. But their beloved customers and friends have rallied to support them.

Pablo Alvarado continues to lead the National Day Laborer Organizing Network, but, as Gavin Newsom predicted to me after our interview, some of the migrant workers for whom Alvarado fights and who would be central to the rebuilding effort have been targeted by the Trump administration.

On McNally Avenue, in Altadena, Herb and Loyda Wilson were let back onto their property after about a week and a half of being stuck outside the perimeter.

"She almost went every day," Herb told me about Loyda over lunch at a deli in nearby Eagle Rock, where they were temporarily living. "And then when she didn't go every day, she went every week until they cleared the property. She was looking for a wedding ring."

They didn't find it, but they did find a little tile that had sat in the kitchen of their home. "It said, 'God doesn't send you through troubled waters to drown you, but to cleanse you.'"

Loyda told me about her reaction upon finding it. "God, thank you for talking to me, because I know you are here for us."

They intend to rebuild. Some of their neighbors do not, having already listed their lots—cleared by the Army Corps of Engineers and inspected by the Environmental Protection Agency—for sale. Cate Heneghan isn't one of them. She, too, with her brother, dug through her home's remains and found an important family heirloom.

"It was a brooch, and it had melted. It was, you know, mostly silver. There's a little bit of gold, a little bit of platinum in there, and it just all melted together. It was on the mantle, and it had fallen off the mantle and onto the floor," hidden among Batchelder tile. The brooch had been designed to celebrate the marriage of their mother and father, descendants of Irish immigrants.

"He pulled up one tile, and he pulled up another, and there it was. It had melted in between because, you know, the hearth is a hundred years old. We knew exactly what it was."

Heneghan's pride in Altadena is matched by so many of her neighbors.

"I tried to brag about my block to somebody once," she told me over an herbal tea near JPL, "and they were like, 'Yeah, yeah, yeah, my block is the same.'"

The intersection of pride and recovery is also something those who answered the call are struggling to work through fully. When I met this spring with firefighters Jake Torres and Gunner Alves and Captain Joshua Swaney, they were still at work in Altadena, in the foothills of the San Gabriel Mountains for the Los Angeles County Fire Department. In the kitchen at Twelves, the captain told me what it's like to fight fires today without the landscape that was once so familiar.

"You don't realize how much you drive by landmarks," Swaney reflected. "Like, you talk about recognizing an intersection and then completely not recognizing an intersection. You're like, 'Oh, hey, we take a right at the school. Oh, the school ain't there!'" he shared. "Drive over to Elevens. I mean, you're obviously, you saw street names, but you're like, 'Oh, I take a right at the blue house,' and you don't even realize you take a right at the blue house every time."

All these months later, it's still hard to process.

"And you're like, it's a war zone," Captain Swaney said. "And you're all like, how is this in Los Angeles right now?"

In the Palisades, firefighters Eric Mendoza of Sixty-Nines and Tim Larson of Twenty-Threes are still hard at work, too. And displaced residents are coming by to check on them.

"You know, even now, like, you see people, and they're trying to rehouse," Larson told me. "People come by, and they thank us. 'What do you need?'"

Mendoza told me what it was like to meet President Trump when he came to Sixty-Nines after he was sworn in. (More on that in a minute.)

"It was one of those love, hate, because the president's here. It's awesome. But all of us inside, we look around, and it's like we lost," he said of the devastation around them. "And still now they're doing cancer research on us. I know that."

"Are you worried about that?" I asked.

"A little bit, yeah," he admitted. "I told my wife and, you know, my kids . . . That's what I signed up for. I know it's a job and, you know, but it's just. It's. It's part of the job."

Firefighters from Northern California who had participated in the mutual-aid effort also had their blood tested, and showed elevated levels of lead and mercury, three and five times higher, respectively, than a control group of firefighters, the *Los Angeles Times* reported.

"What you need to worry about is some of these metals that, when they get burned, they get up in the air," project researcher Dr. Kari Nadeau, chair of the Department of Environmental Health at Harvard T. H. Chan School of Public Health, told the paper. "They can get into your lungs, and they can get into your skin, and they can get absorbed and get into your blood."

In August 2025 Hannah Dreier published in *The New York Times* a chronicle of the devastating diseases faced by wildland firefighters because of exposure to toxic smoke—including heart and lung disease and, as Nick Schuler of Cal Fire feared in the Palisades, cancer.

The fires also reopened deep emotional fault lines that are a key part of, if not unique to, Los Angeles's identity.

"What is most distinctive about Los Angeles is not simply its conjugation of earthquakes, wildfires, and floods," Mike Davis wrote in his book *Ecology of Fear* in 1998, "but its uniquely explosive mixture of natural hazards and social contradictions."

Whether the Palisades, largely white and affluent, or Altadena, historically working class and far more diverse, can rebuild their homes and lives will also be a function of the political power they are able to marshal. Inequality has always been a feature of disaster response in Los Angeles—see Davis's historic documentation of separate and unequal response to fire disasters in Los Angeles's wage-earning and immigrant communities. It's why he famously wrote "The Case for Letting Malibu Burn," an article for the journal *Environmental History Review* in 1995.

What's *new* about America's current age of disaster is that we are living through one in which, as Captain White implored me to consider, disinformation is making naturally occurring catastrophes and the forces that exacerbate them even worse. The Eaton Fire and the Palisades Fires ushered in the most acute and latest chapter of this new age because of their proximity to the second inauguration of Donald J. Trump as president of the United States.

Gavin Newsom got an early preview of President Trump's willingness to politicize and distort disaster for his own perceived gain shortly after he was sworn in for his second term. It was a beautiful blue-sky day at Los Angeles International Airport on Friday January 24, 2025. California's governor was standing below Air Force One, the legendary Boeing 747 painted in blue, white, and gold, that had just carried President Donald Trump on his first trip of his second term. After the plane stopped rolling and the stairs were pulled up to the front door, Newsom stood, hands in his back pockets. He appeared to be wearing the same blue button-down shirt, jeans, and desert boots he was wearing when I last saw him.

Newsom seemed fidgety, standing alone with no other greeters for the president, as the seconds turned to minutes ticking by without Trump emerging, leaving Newsom to look around, up at Air Force One, back at Marine One behind him, and to pivot around as the time passed. There was good reason: Despite formal outreach to President Trump, Newsom did not appear on his official schedule and had been invited only at the very last minute to stand at the bottom of the stairs as Trump arrived.

That morning, Newsom had directed his staff to follow up with the White House about the forty-seventh president's visit when the schedule came out.

"Can you just call the White House and say, 'Look, no shenanigans.' I just think it's appropriate. Happy to say hello. I'm really happy he's here."

Then again, with a couple of hours to go, Newsom asked his team to try one last time as President Trump was flying to LA from North Carolina, where he had first surveyed the lingering wind and flood damage from the previous fall's Hurricane Helene. This time it was a yes, albeit a tepid one, with the Trump people saying essentially, "If you want to show up, show up."

So Newsom did. As he waited at the bottom of the rolling staircase, he didn't know if he was walking into a setup for the president to berate "Newscum."

An aide approached and told the governor the plan. Newsom spoke with Trump's advance man, establishing that the conversation with Trump would be a quick hello, without press, and the First Lady would join them before they departed on Marine One for the Palisades.

As Newsom stood there looking like someone waiting for an Uber, he thought about what it must look like to the long lens cameras pointed at him, as he recalled to me during a lengthy conversation inside his Sacramento office in May 2025.

They probably put me out to have that image of the lonely guy there, he groused. *Okay, this is all part of the shtick, but I'm fine. Like, this is good. We need to do this. It's not about the Newsom guy and this Trump guy. It's about the goddamn president and the governor of California and people that are literally in need, suffering, and they need to see us get along.*

Trump emerged from the door of the giant plane first, wearing a suit topped with his white button-down open to the second button and complemented by a black and gold MAGA hat. Melania followed, in a tan trench with the collar popped and a black ballcap of her own and a pair of aviators. Trump glanced toward the Pacific Ocean and Marine One to his right, and then descended the stairs. When he reached the fifth step from the top, he looked up, and with his right hand waved and then flashed a thumbs-up to Newsom.

This feels so familiar, the governor thought.

At the bottom of the stairs, Trump and Newsom both extended their right hands for a shake, and placed their left hands on each other's right shoulders to pull each other in. It wasn't a hug, but it was close. Newsom flashed a megawatt smile as they backed away from each other, but he didn't let go of Trump's hand. For twelve seconds they looked directly into each other's eyes and spoke.

"Mr. President, I just want to thank you for being here," Newsom said to Trump. "And you know what? We need to work this out." On the cameras you could see Newsom say, "I'm serious."

"We worked out in COVID all this stuff," Newsom continued.

"Well," Trump replied, "we've got to do the water."

Looking directly at President Trump, Newsom replied, "Yeah, we clearly haven't figured that one out, the two of us."

"Hey, you want to meet with the press?" the president asked the governor. Before Newsom had a chance to reply, Trump made a beeline for the assembled media, and Newsom reached over and gave the First Lady a kiss on the cheek. They both followed Trump toward the cameras.

"We're going to be taking a little tour with some of the people from the area," the president said about the Palisades after a quick update about his visit to North Carolina. "I appreciate the governor coming out and meeting me, Gavin." They shook hands again.

"Thank you very much," Trump went on. "And, again, we'll be talking a little bit later. We want to get it fixed. We want to get the problem fixed. And there'll be some ways. It's like you got hit by a bomb, right?"

"Yeah."

"It's like you got hit by a bomb. Would you like to say something? Go ahead."

"Most importantly," Newsom began, "thank you for being here. Means a great deal to all of us. Not just the folks in Palisades. The folks in Altadena that were devastated. We're going to need your support."

"Yeah," Trump said.

"We're gonna need your help. You were there for us during COVID," Newsom said again, this time for the cameras as Trump smirked. "I don't forget that. I have all the expectations that we'll be able to work together to get this speedy recovery."

"We will. We're gonna get it done. A tremendous number of lives have been affected. A *lot* of real estate has been affected. Nobody has ever, probably, seen anything like this," the president postulated.

"No," Newsom interjected.

"You can almost say since the Second World War, when you think of it." Trump shrugged and waved his hands at hip level. "Nothing like this has happened. And we're going to get it fixed. We're going to get it permanently fixed so it can't happen again. And we're going to be talking about it a little later and we'll get it worked out," he said, looking Newsom in the eye. "OK?"

"I appreciate it, Mr. President," Newsom offered while shaking hands and patting Trump on the back.

"Thank you, Governor."

One of the assembled reporters asked President Trump about what she called "a lot" of disagreements about what had happened regarding the fire and the response.

"We gotta get it finished. We're looking to get something completed. And the way you get it completed is to work together. He's the governor of this state. And we're going to get it completed, they're going to need a lot of federal help. Unless you don't need any, which would be OK," Trump said, smiling.

"We're going to need a lot of federal help," Newsom replied, again tapping Trump's back.

Trump and Newsom thanked the reporters and turned away from them.

"I'll see you . . ." Trump said to Newsom as they stepped out of range of the audio feed, walking toward Marine One. As they approached the Sikorsky VH-3D Sea King, Trump continued the conversation.

"Let's go," he told Newsom, gesturing for him to board the chopper. "I guess we're having a roundtable."

"I'm not having a roundtable," said Newsom, puzzled because he hadn't been invited to take part in one. "What are you talking about? I don't even know what you have organized."

This is awkward, Newsom thought about the predicament he found himself in. *Nobody from my team is here. The Secret Service knocked them out. And if I go, I don't know where I'm going to end up. Will anyone find me? He's not going to take me back up. He's just going to drop me off and we could be anywhere.* He decided not to get on the chopper.

"Hey, thanks for coming out," he said to the president.

"We're going to be good. We're good," Trump said, repeating a line he frequently uses with Newsom. "I'm going to call you later tonight."

With that, Newsom bid the Trumps adieu, and they took off on an aerial tour of the Palisades, landing to walk a street blocks away from the destroyed home of Stephen Miller's parents, and holding an at-times contentious roundtable with local officials, including Los Angeles Mayor Karen Bass and Trump's hand-picked envoy to the fire zone, Richard Grenell, the former acting director of national intelligence. (Trump did not visit Altadena.)

That night, Trump kept his promise and called Newsom, he told me, but the governor, not recognizing the number, sent Trump to voicemail. When he listened to it, it was Trump's recap of the roundtable in the Palisades—which had been a disaster for local officials, who were steamrolled by the president's continuing to insist that the solution to fires was to open a mystical tap to send water flowing into Southern California.

"We want to get that water pouring down here as quickly as possible and let hundreds of millions of gallons of water flow down into Southern California, and that'll be a big benefit to you. Look, if you don't want it, you're going to tell me, but just—I can't imagine it," he bullied them.

"It pours down naturally. It has for a million years, for a million years. It pours down. You'll never run out. You'll never have shortages, and you'll—you won't have things like this. And when you do, you'll have a lot of water to put it out. So, I'm going to ask that you figure that out, but I am . . . I really, strongly recommended this seven years ago, and I think I'm going to just do it."

Trump, later in the event, came up with the idea of doing away with reservoirs altogether.

"You know, you don't even need reservoirs," he declared. "With the water coming down, you don't need the reservoir. You have so much water. You don't need it. You only have reservoirs because you tried to hold water. But you have natural water coming down along the coast. For a million years, it's been coming. You know that, right?"

On January 30, twenty-three days after ignition of the Eaton and Palisades Fires, and the day before they were fully contained, the Army Corps of Engineers, at the direction of the White House, began releasing what the president claimed was over one billion gallons of water into the Central Valley from two reservoirs—*not* to Southern California but to fields that didn't need or weren't prepared for the deluge. According to *The Washington Post*, the wasted flow would have been "enough water to supply as many as 7,000 California households for a year."

Wasting an eventual two-and-a-half billion gallons of water was a Trump sideshow to the damage that would soon be inflicted by his administration on the federal government's ability to respond to natural disasters.

Trump's decimation of the federal workforce through his Department of Government Efficiency directly impaired the ability to respond to wildfires, too. In the weeks after the inauguration, I met

Ben McLane, a firefighting captain with the US Forest Service. Before his time in the Gifford Pinchot National Forest, named for the first chief of the US Forest Service, McLane had served as an elite hotshot firefighter in Lake County, California. Months earlier, a study in the journal *Nature Ecology and Evolution* found that "extreme wildfire events during the past two decades more than doubled in frequency and magnitude globally," with "the six worst seasons occurring during the past seven years," according to the news website Axios. And this was before the Great Los Angeles Fires broke out.

I interviewed McLane in February 2025 at the site of the 2023 Tunnel 5 Fire in Washington state, which burned over five hundred acres. "I have firefighters who I should be bringing on, and I'm not able to because our HR practices have stopped until the hiring freeze is lifted, or they're given permission to continue," he told me, as a winter storm dumped snow on both of us. "It's as simple as that."

In addition, potential cuts to NASA's Earth Sciences Division put at risk missions designed specifically to better understand and fight the fires of the future—just like the Great Los Angeles Fires. In April 2025 I joined NASA, the Defense Department, and the Interior Department on the FireSense mission, an effort to study the science of wildfire using imaging spectrometry on controlled burns.

"We're trying to combine all aspects of the fire life cycle and using science to understand what is happening and what we can do about it," Harrison Raine, a former hotshot firefighter and now a project coordinator for NASA, told me. With their program on the potential chopping block, to add insult to injury, Raine's colleagues Holly Bender and Daniel Jensen, with whom I flew as they used the imaging spectrometer to map the fire in real time, all work for Jet Propulsion Laboratory, based at Caltech. More than two hundred and fifty JPL and other Caltech employees, including engineer Cate Heneghan, lost their homes in the Eaton Fire.

In May 2025, as FEMA worked to deliver relief to the victims of the fires, it hemorrhaged career senior officials as political appointees refashioned the agency by slashing key hires that respond to disasters, leading one FEMA employee to tell me, "It's like having a relay team, and instead of having six members, you've only got four, and, yeah, you can do it, but those four runners are going to have to run more than they're trained for."

The National Weather Service and the National Oceanic and Atmospheric Administration, where Dr. Ariel Cohen and Dave Gomberg warned about the particularly dangerous situation that led to the fires, lost a thousand employees to layoffs, including meteorologists. The cuts affect the agency's ability to forecast accurately. When I visited both of them in May 2025, a whiteboard featured six bullet points written there by their colleague.

- Trust yourself + your team
- Prioritize your physical + mental health
- Extend grace to yourself and others
- Our work is essential. We make a difference every day!
- Stay confident, keep moving forward
- Uncertainty is inevitable. We have the power to choose resilience, adaptability + commitment

As the *Los Angeles Times* reported in June 2025, "At least two weather service offices in California no longer have enough staff to operate overnight: Sacramento and Hanford, which together cover the Central Valley and the Sierra, among the state's most fire-prone regions." That same month, President Trump threatened to withhold disaster aid from California because of pushback from Governor Newsom about the administration's wide scale and ongoing immigration enforcement operations in Los Angeles. The operations were sweeping up undocumented residents without violent criminal records from all walks of life, such as landscapers, farmers (including those in the fields around the National Weather Service's office in Oxnard), and the same day laborers who were working to rebuild the city.

Asked whether Newsom's posture against the raids might adversely influence federal funding, the president said bluntly, "It could impact. You know, hatred is never a good thing in politics. When you don't like somebody, you don't respect somebody, it's harder for that person to get money if you're on top."

That operation was the brainchild of Stephen Miller, whose parents' home burned down in the Palisades. He'd quite possibly first learned about the tragic news from my visit at the request of his wife, Katie. Despite her outreach during the fire, and what I thought might be a thaw in our adversarial professional relationship, it didn't last. Katie Miller and I have not talked since, and a text message I sent her during the transition asking for guidance on forthcoming executive orders was rebuffed.

Katie Miller did, however, eventually speak publicly about the fires. On the day charges were filed against the alleged arsonist who started the blaze that prosecutors say rekindled to become the Palisades Fire, Miller posted a message on social media. "You mean . . . It wasn't climate change?"

The day I unsuccessfully messaged Katie Miller hoping to learn more about Trump's plans was the day my own dad was named chief recovery officer of the City of Los Angeles's efforts to rebuild Pacific Palisades. (Altadena was outside the city's jurisdiction, and its rebuilding would be a separate effort.) After his career in public service was launched by fixing up our park in

1986, he served in different capacities—inside and outside of government—for five Los Angeles mayors, coming close to becoming mayor himself in 2001. His tenure as chief recovery officer was short, though: ninety days, and not immune to the slings and arrows of local politics.

Despite early and continuing discord about the recovery, as a son and Angeleno, it was a point of pride and full-circle moment for our family. From my dad's 1986 effort with my mom to create a playground in the Palisades, to a press conference in 2025 in front of the plaque marking it that survived the fire, he became intimately involved with all levels of government and civil society—from working with the Army Corps of Engineers on debris removal, to helping find a temporary location for Palisades High School. I am in awe of him and his work, and for reentering the arena after decades as a fixture in civic life. His desire to be a part of the solution embodied to me his decades of devoted public service to Los Angeles, a city that we as a family have never loved more. He's my role model.

The fires were not just a political football—or fuel for disinformation. Real and profound grief and anger of affected residents who continue to speak out to this day was almost immediately trained on local politicians—like the resident who accosted Governor Newsom the same day I ran into him in the Palisades as he tried to get President Biden on the phone—and Mayor Bass, who became the subject of a recall effort funded by Robert F. Kennedy Jr.'s former presidential running mate. Her fire chief, Crowley, of the LAFD, lost her job after, as the fires burned, publicly calling out the Mayor's budgeting as a limiting factor in the department's response. Bass said she removed Crowley because of her performance before and during the fire, including sending home firefighters on duty the morning of January 7, and a failure to notify her directly of the danger the city was facing. An investigation by the *Los Angeles Times* "found that LAFD officials did not pre-deploy any engines to the Palisades ahead of the Jan. 7 fire, despite warnings about extreme weather. In preparing for the winds, the department staffed up only five of more than 40 engines available to supplement the regular firefighting force."

The mop-up is the process by which firefighters stamp out hotspots, ensuring the fire is out once and for all. The spirit of a mop-up also extends, albeit less definitionally, to the efforts of academics, scientists, and public officials who work to reduce harm in the wake of these disasters and find ways to avoid the worst of the pain they cause in the future. But in America's New Age of Disaster, what a mop-up looks like—how we understand disasters that have unfolded—is being challenged by politics.

Captain White warned me about this. His framework about how to think of these Great Los Angeles Fires—that what I experienced was the confluence of deteriorating infrastructure, changes in the way we live, climate change, and misinformation and disinformation—has greatly shaped my thinking.

As I wrote and reported this book, examples of each were not only easy to find—they were the entire story.

The aboveground utilities.

The electric car batteries exploding.

The bone-dry conditions.

Infrastructure not suited for a massive community conflagration.

And the overwhelming and constant deluge of false information about the fires' causes and ways to mitigate them going forward.

White retired from the federal government at the end of September 2025. He now intends to fight back against the fires of the future not from within the Department of Health and Human Services, where he served as a member of the US Public Health Service Commissioned Corps for most of his career. He has declared a run for Congress in his home state of Maryland. And he's not the only one for whom the fires were a catalyst to potential future elected office.

Jake Levine, the Biden White House aide whose mom lost her home in the Palisades, has declared to run for Congress, too, challenging longtime incumbent Brad Sherman, a Democrat, who, at the Palisades roundtable convened by Trump, sparred with the newly sworn-in POTUS in an uncomfortable and unproductive made-for-TV spat.

Levine said the fires made it "clear that our politicians are falling short—not just on climate, but on the basics." On Capitol Hill, both he and White hope to find the power to extinguish the inferno of disinformation and innuendo about how and why Los Angeles burned. But it was outside the National Institute of Occupational Safety and Health (NIOSH) in April 2025 that I saw where the true power lies.

On a street corner in Morgantown, West Virginia, I spoke with federal government employees and their supporters who had been or were in the crosshairs of losing their jobs due to the Trump administration and Elon Musk's self-described chainsaw approach to trimming government bureaucracy—including in support roles for firefighters.

On a beautiful sunny day, the protestors held signs, including ones that described how "NIOSH works for miners, firefighters, and all American workers," as drivers-by honked to make literal noise about the cuts.

Among the key research that had been slated for elimination: programs within the Center for Firefighter Safety, Health, and Well-being. In the face of the decimation of the program and others that worked to protect the health and well-being of first responders who were called to duty at disasters like the one that had unfolded in Los Angeles, the courage of the NIOSH protestors, the support for their efforts by the American people, and, ultimately, their local politicians' voices reversed the firings, at least temporarily.

Watching your hometown burn down is not something I would wish on anyone. But in the wake of these Great Los Angeles Fires, I have had the privilege of seeing up close how the natural catastrophes faced in America's New Age of Disaster cannot be fought by first responders alone. Ordinary people—the workers of the United States—are today as much a last line of defense in America's New Age of Disaster as the brave men and women on whom we have for so long relied.

On day-laborer corners in Altadena, workers rebuilding Los Angeles after the fires are holding regular rallies against Trump's raids meant to deport them and stop their work.

In the skies above controlled burns across the country, NASA earth scientists are studying ways to better fight fires in the face of ongoing climate change, despite the fact the current administration has signaled it does not want them to utter the phrase.

And along the winding Monongahela River in Morgantown, public health professionals and their allies are standing up not only to defend their own jobs but also to save the lives of those who might one day save theirs.

In disaster, hope often emerges. And it is in the people, not the politics, I found it after the Great Los Angeles Fires of 2025.

Acknowledgments

THANK YOU, LOS ANGELES. THE PEOPLE, THE PLACES, the landscape. My home. Our home.

Thank you to my sources, experts in their fields, proud Altadenans and Palisadians, brave first responders and more—both named and unnamed in these pages—whose stories and knowledge are the backbone of this book.

Thank you to Peter Hubbard, Maureen Cole, and the entire team at Mariner Books and HarperCollins for another extraordinary partnership that enabled me to dive deeper, learn more, and share what I experienced in real time.

Thank you to Alan Berger and Mollie Glick at CAA for helping make this book a reality.

Thank you to Billy Brennan, for your fact-checking.

Thank you to countless local reporters, especially my friends at KNBC, for exemplary coverage of this disaster and its aftermath that was and continues to be the definition of journalism in the public interest. I am in awe of you all.

Thank you to everyone at NBC News and MSNBC for the best ten professional years of my life, which have allowed me to tell stories that matter about real people with lives far afield from the studios in New York and Washington, and for your support of this project. I'm so proud of the work we've done together and will continue to do at MS NOW.

Thank you to my hometown friends, who were there for me at all hours to offer support and love during the fires, and after when I would call to mine their memories of what we all went through together.

And thank you, most importantly, to my extraordinary family, for whom Los Angeles is as much a part of our DNA as our genetics: my mom and dad, my brother and three sisters, in-laws, niece and nephews, and, at the top of my list, my wife, Nicole; son, Noah; and daughter, Lucia. I want you to know how much I appreciate the amount you all sacrificed—during the fires and after—to enable me to go on this journey. This book is dedicated to my fellow Angelenos, including and especially to you. I love you.

Notes on Sourcing

THIS BOOK IS THE PRODUCT OF DOZENS OF HOURS OF conversations over many months with sources whose stories you read about here. While constructed as scenes, when quoted directly or as *italicized thoughts*, the words attributed to characters in this book were based on what they told me—their recollection of events and what was said as directly described to me, or in the case of my own dialogue, as I recall it or review it from reporting that aired live on television. I acknowledge that others may recall these events or conversations differently.

The work I did in real time for NBC News and MSNBC is all recorded and was used as source material when describing live reporting I did on air. I also relied on the extraordinary work of other journalists. The text messages between fire chiefs were discovered in a public records request by the Los Angeles affiliate of ABC News, which also did reporting that proved critical to my understanding of the Eaton Fire's ignition. The *Los Angeles Times*, too, has done meticulous work on what happened beneath those steel towers that night. The Palisades Fire's ignition wasn't witnessed by human eyes, but the *San Francisco Chronicle* was able to obtain key video evidence from the University of California, and it informed my writing about those moments. And as you saw throughout this book, the multiday-around-the-clock reporting of my colleagues at KNBC was nothing short of heroic, and without their work, the people of Southern California—and certainly readers of this book—wouldn't have had anywhere near the visibility into what was happening, when, and how.

So many of the issues I touch on in this book are deserving of more inquiry and ink. I highly recommend, for starters, Basel Musharbash's report, for the newsletter *BIG* from Matt Stoller, examination of private equity's role in the replacement and repair of so many of the fire trucks that sat in that maintenance yard in LA during the blazes; Mike Baker's *New York Times* report about why the Santa Ynez Reservoir was offline during the fires; a piece for the *Los Angeles Times* by Melody Petersen and Jenny Jarvie about SoCal Edison's delay in inspecting high-voltage aboveground transmission lines before the Eaton Fire; Rebecca Ellis's work, also for the *Los Angeles Times*, on the emergency alert system and its connection to fatalities in West Altadena; an investigation by her colleagues Paul Pringle, Alene Tchekmedyian, and Dakota Smith into why the Los Angeles City Fire Department didn't pre-position more assets in the Palisades ahead of the fire; and Tony Briscoe, Noah Haggerty, and Haley Smith's work, also for the *Los Angeles Times*, about the federal government's refusing to pay for soil testing in the fire's aftermath. Ongoing investigations and legal battles around insurance—dropping Californians ahead of the fire and denial of claims—will also be consequential, as is Hannah Dreier's investigation into deadly diseases afflicting wildland firefighters and the political interference into potential solutions.

While all of these factors may have contributed to or exacerbated the particularly dangerous situation that was the fire's most identifiable cause, I recommend watching or reading the February 2025 opening statement to the House Judiciary Committee's Subcommittee of the Administrative State, Regulatory Reform and Antitrust Committee by Frank Frievalt, the director of the Wildland-Urban Interface Fire Institute at the California Polytechnic State University (Cal Poly), for a better understanding of the complexity of these fires of the future, especially for those battling them. I have enjoyed, too, listening and subscribing to *The HotShot Wake Up* newsletter and podcast, for a near real-time feed of what wildland firefighters face daily. Ben McLane of the US Forest Service is one of those firefighters, and as a conversation develops nationally yet again about consolidating the federal fighting agencies, McLane's writings—especially about what values-based leadership looks like in wildland fire agencies—has made a profound impact on my understanding of the noble profession.

Text messages, photographs, and conversations with my colleagues from NBC News with whom I reported in the field also provided important refreshers and context for what we experienced together—particularly Bianca Seward's efforts to retrace our steps in the fire's earliest hours.

The journalist William Brennan fact-checked the stories within these pages against the audio recordings and transcripts of my interviews, and for details I describe when reporting on the science, characteristics, and details of the fires themselves and where they took place.

Index